Praise for *Finding Faith in the Dark*

Finding Faith in the Dark is filled with stories of people who *want* to believe when their worlds seem not to support belief. That's the world where real people find the real God. You may find your story here too.

—JOHN ORTBERG, senior pastor of Menlo Park
Presbyterian Church, Menlo Park, California, and author of
If You Want to Walk on Water, You've Got to Get Out of the Boat

I've seen Laurie in action at a Youth Specialties convention and at her church. After hearing her seesaw account of life as a single, and now married, woman, I urged her to write her story. I thought it would encourage many others.

—PHILIP YANCEY, award-winning author of *The Jesus
I Never Knew* and *What's So Amazing about Grace?*

Laurie Short has been following Jesus into places of light and of darkness—because all of that is part of being an authentic person and a genuine disciple. Here she reflects on lessons she has seen in her life and in the lives of others. Let her honesty of faith lead and encourage your own.

—MARK LABBERTON,
president of Fuller Theological Seminary

There are certain books you read, and certain books you experience as you read. *Finding Faith in the Dark* leads us to experience the truth that there is purpose in the plans we never pick, because there is a God who chooses to use any plan for his good. I'm grateful for a book that doesn't give easy answers to hard questions but leads us to experience the One whose presence always provides just enough light to know we are never alone.

—HELEN MUSICK, transformation pastor at
Quest Community Church, Lexington, Kentucky

This book will be unbelievably helpful to so many people who are eager to know that Someone helped them find a sure and steady hand on their shoulder—guiding them to all the right places and all the right people. Faith comes to some of us when we least expect it—even when it is dark and our footing is unsure. I can't tell you how joyful I am that Laurie wrote this book for people like me, and maybe for you. It is this guidance we need to find the very path that will lead us to exactly where we need and want to go.

—NEIL CLARK WARREN, founder and CEO of Eharmony.com and author of *Finding the Love of your Life*

Finding Faith in the Dark is Laurie Short's amazingly inspiring story of finding hope and joy in the midst of broken dreams. Actually, it's everyone's story. You will find beauty and meaning on every page. Laurie writes with the same authenticity she daily lives out. She is a masterful storyteller, and you will feel like you're sitting across from her as she mentors you and gives you strength. Find a quiet spot, and get ready to be encouraged.

—JIM BURNS, PhD, president of HomeWord and author of *Confident Parenting*

As we navigate our Christian lives in a broken and upside-down reality, this book provides the hope that God is still working thru our situations in amazing ways. Allow this resource to bless you and equip you to find God within your trials.

—REV. EFREM SMITH, president and CEO of World Impact and author of *The Post-Black and Post-White Church*

If you need to hear how faith can deepen when your prayers aren't answered the way you had hoped, Laurie's book is the one to read. She shares from wisdom she has earned. It's a story that will keep you reading to the last page. This is a book to savor.

—PAULA RINEHART, author of *Sex and the Soul of a Woman*

FINDING FAITH
in the
DARK

WHEN *the* STORY *of* YOUR LIFE TAKES *a* TURN
YOU DIDN'T PLAN

LAURIE SHORT

ZONDERVAN®

ZONDERVAN

Finding Faith in the Dark
Copyright © 2014 by Laurie Short

This title is also available as a Zondervan ebook. Visit www.zondervan.com/ebooks.

ISBN 978-0-310-33708-9 (ebook)

Requests for information should be addressed to:

Zondervan, 3900 *Sparks Drive SE Grand Rapids, Michigan 49546*

Library of Congress Cataloging-in-Publication Data

Short, Laurie, 1972–
    Finding faith in the dark : when the story of your life takes a turn you didn't
    plan / Laurie Short.—1st [edition].
        pages cm
    ISBN 978-0-310-33711-9 (softcover)
    1. Faith. 2. Trust in God. 3. Expectation (Psychology)—Religious
    aspects—Christianity. I. Title.
    BV4637.S48 2014
    234'.23—dc23   2013041257

Published in association with the literary agency of WordServe Literary Group, Ltd.,
10152 S. Knoll Circle, Highlands Ranch, CO 80130 (www.wordserveliterary.com).

Cover design: James Hall
Cover photo: Shutterstock®
Interior design: Katherine Lloyd, The DESK

First printing June 2014 / Printed in the United States of America

Jun-29-2014

94356_CRC_1403

To Jere and Jordan Short,
God's great story for my life.
You mean more to me than you will ever know.

Contents

IV. WHEN GRACE FILTERS THROUGH

Part I

FAITH IN THE DARK

I said to the man who stood at the gate of the year,
"Give me a light so that I may tread safely into the
unknown!"
And he replied, "Go into the darkness and put your
hand into the hand of God.
That shall be to you better than a known light and
safer than a known way."

—Minnie Louise Haskins, "The Gate of the Year"

CHAPTER I

WHERE YOU DO NOT WANT TO GO

In the first book of the Bible, we find a curious story. The patriarch Jacob enters into an all-night wrestling match with an angel of God, locks him in a hold, and then whispers, "I will not let you go unless you bless me" (Genesis 32:26).

The audaciousness of Jacob's request is only surpassed by the surprise of what happens next. The angel does what Jacob asks. He reaches out and touches Jacob, the searing power of his finger leaving a limp in Jacob's body and penetrating his soul.

Jacob wanted what only God could give — the really good things, the blessings. But Jacob's blessing came with something he hadn't asked for, and that limp was what changed him.

Our own experiences of wrestling with God rarely happen in one night, as it did for Jacob. Sometimes they happen over years — even decades — as we try to figure out what God is doing, why that blessing we were counting on isn't coming the way we hoped. Maybe you've been there.

The husband or wife you prayed for never came.

The husband or wife you stayed faithful to had an affair.

The death of a spouse or child tore your heart.

A parent's abuse or addiction damaged your life.

A diagnosis took away your health and your future.

When these things happen, we are left wondering, "Where is that God who promises to answer our prayers if we delight in him? Why isn't my life turning out the way I hoped, let alone how I had planned?"

If you've ever been somewhere in life you don't want to be, this book is for you. And more than helping you find your way out of that place, my hope is that this book will help you find your way *in* that place, because I believe there is something that place has to give you. Hope springs from the fact that our story is never finished until we leave this earth. Something can always happen.

That's why you have to hold on. God can show up where you least expect him to be.

In May 2012, Kim posted on her Facebook page that her Westmont sabbatical had officially begun. Her husband, Ken, took her on a seven-day cruise. They happily ate their way through Puerto Vallarta, and Kim thought her stomach pain was probably a reaction to the rich food and wobbly deck. When they got back, they found out it wasn't the food or the deck. Kim had Stage IV ovarian cancer.

Ken had made a list of things they wanted to do while

Kim was on sabbatical. Surgery and chemotherapy took their unwelcome place at the top of the list. Eventually, they became the list. Kim faced surgery like a champ, but the prospect of losing her thick blonde hair became the tipping point for her tears. Ken promised to spare no expense on a beautiful wig, and he held her as she cried. It was a symbol of a greater loss, as they said good-bye to the life they formerly knew. Cancer would be their new normal.

It seemed like an unfair turn of events for a couple who had only recently gotten back on their feet. Three and a half years earlier, their home burned to the ground in a devastating fire. They had lived in their new home for just two years. At the time of the fire, they were accompanying a group of students on a semester abroad in Europe, and when they received word that their home was gone, they had just finished a tour of Auschwitz. With images of the Nazi prison camp fresh in their minds, Ken remembers whispering to Kim, "We may not have our pictures, but we have the people in our pictures." As Ken gazed at his bride before her first chemotherapy, he realized in a new way what a blessing that was.

Ken wished he could take his wife's place as she bravely faced the violent nausea that accompanied each treatment. Holding her as she vomited, Ken thought back to the perspective he gained in Auschwitz. He decided that wherever this journey would take them, he would be grateful for every day they had.

Ken stood by Kim's side as she went through twenty-four rounds of chemotherapy. He loved her when she was in pain. He loved her when she became bald. He loved her when she couldn't leave her bed. Kim's Facebook postings went up and down with her chart, but her faith never waned. Her unyielding optimism cheered Ken on in their battle. In the middle of her postings, Kim wrote, "I am thankful to have a husband who shows me every day how much God loves me."

Though Ken prays every morning for his wife's health to be restored, they are both aware the cancer could take her. There are days when the pain is so immense that she almost wishes it would. Nevertheless they treasure each day and shoulder this trial with a mysterious sense that God has never been so close.

Ken says he has discovered things about his love for Kim that he never would have known had it not been for the cancer. And for that, he is grateful. Ken and Kim have gone where they didn't want to go. But it is evident that God is with them.

When Marla married a youth pastor, she had many visions for how her life would unfold. Becoming a single mother was not one of them. Her husband had proposed by taking her up in a plane, and as they looked down, he pointed to a marching band that had spelled out the words "Will you marry me?" After he instructed her to read the words out loud, he was the one who said yes.

His charisma had followed him throughout his life, and he seemed poised for a long and successful ministry career. Because Marla had a deep desire to serve God, she was thrilled to be his teammate.

In the months that followed her storybook wedding, a

young woman came forward who had been in her husband's youth group. Apparently there had been an "incident." Unsure what to believe, the church came to its youth pastor's defense. It wasn't until three other women came forward that the truth of what had happened started to become clear.

As the story broke, Marla saw her life crashing down in front of her. She thought she had married a pastor. Instead she had married a sex abuser.

When her husband was let go from his position and told to enter rehabilitation, he was remorseful and heartbroken. Bravely, Marla stayed with him. For one year, she lived with him in an apartment complex, complying with the treatment of daily therapy sessions and processing the reality that ministry was no longer an option for their future. Grace surprised her when, after the year had passed, they received a call from a church three states away. This church had known both of them for many years and was aware of the delicate journey they'd been on. The church's leaders were willing to give Marla's husband another chance if he was open to serve in a different capacity under intense accountability. As Marla moved away from family and friends, she thanked God that they had been given a fresh start.

Months passed, and they started settling in, meeting new friends and enjoying life in their new community. As things stabilized, Marla was thrilled to discover she was pregnant. Three weeks after Marla gave birth to their baby boy, her husband came home with an empty look on his face.

"Well, you might as well know it's happened again," he said in a voice just above a whisper. He took the blanket off their bed and slept on the couch.

As those dreaded words replayed over and over in her mind, Marla lay paralyzed in the silence. A strange mixture of guilt, remorse, and heartbreak washed over her. The following week, she took their baby, got on a plane, and went home to her family.

Two years later, Marla's marriage ended with a signature.

After the birth of her child and the breakup of her marriage, Marla was offered a youth ministry position at a church just a few hours away from where her ex-husband had served. Amazingly, she became a healing agent for the women who had been victims of his illness. In a stroke of painful grace, Marla became the youth pastor she originally thought she had married.

Ten years later, Marla was courted by a thirty-nine-year-old Christian man who had never married and whose sights were set only on her. It took her three years to open her wounded heart. When she and her teenage son finally stood next to her patient suitor at the altar, those of us who witnessed their marriage saw the longevity of faithfulness displayed.

Marla had gone where she didn't want to go. But God was with her.

———◆———

"I've been called to serve in Iraq." It was 2003, and Lisa's fiancé's words fell on her like a dark cloud.

"But you're a reservist," she replied. "I don't understand. Can't you tell them you can't go?"

Lisa thought of spouses who were hearing the very same

words. All over the country, men and women were trying to get their heads and hearts around the news that would alter their families' lives. She was only engaged to a Marine; there were spouses and children who were much more deeply affected by this news. Yet she still couldn't help but feel her own pain.

Lisa was forty-three years old, already past the age of marriage by anyone's standards. She had faithfully prayed for a husband for over twenty years. And then, Lisa met Ryan.

Ryan and Lisa became engaged four months after they met. Ultimately they came to the conclusion that planning a wedding should be secondary to planning a life, and that they needed more time. Their first wedding date was postponed.

After a couple of months and a few therapist bills, they finally set their second date. Ryan and Lisa had to mesh two different personalities, two kids, and an ex-wife, but they were both still on board for a wedding. Lisa had two bridal showers, ordered her bridesmaid dresses, and decided on the most beautiful wedding dress she had ever seen. She hung it in her mom's closet. Now, with the news of Ryan's deployment, it would hang there a lot longer.

In the weeks preceding the deployment, something else disturbed Lisa's thoughts. She thought Ryan's ex-wife might be having second thoughts about their divorce. Lisa consoled herself that Ryan would tell her if anything had changed.

Finally the day arrived for Ryan to be deployed. They all arrived at Camp Pendleton — Ryan, his ex-wife and two kids, and Lisa. Together they waved good-bye, looking like a progressive Hallmark card.

During the first few months of his deployment, her communication with Ryan was pretty steady, but eventually the letters and phone calls tapered off. A military chaplain comforted Lisa by saying Ryan was probably in a place where he couldn't deal too much with life at home. If she loved him, she would wait.

She did. And in the meantime, she turned forty-four.

Nine months later, two days after he returned, they held hands and sat through many pregnant pauses. Then he spoke. "I still love you."

Lisa's heart jumped a little, with a slight twinge of hope that it had all been just a bad dream. "I think I might love you too. Do you still want to get married?"

He paused for a minute, then said, "No." Months later, Lisa found out that Ryan actually *did* want to get married — just not to her. Ryan remarried his ex-wife the year after he returned.

The reason I know this story is because the woman was not named Lisa. It was Laurie. It was me.

When we give up on our story before God has finished writing it, we miss out on what our story has to give us. Sadder still, we miss out on what our story can become.

In the months (and years) that followed my broken engagement, the loss of my dream led to a crossroad of whether or not I would hold on to my faith. In the darkness of disappointment, I struggled. But ultimately I decided to trust — and that choice became the impetus for this book.

That choice also paved the way for the events of my life unfolding in the miraculous way they did. You'll hear later about a new man who eventually changed my name and my life, but at this juncture, let me say this much about story and hope: When we give up on our story before God has finished writing it, we miss out on what our story has to give us. Sadder still, we miss out on what our story can become.

———————————

In John 21, Jesus is talking to Peter, one of his disciples, when suddenly the conversation takes a turn. He says to Peter, "When you were younger you ... went where you wanted; but when you are old ... someone else will ... lead you where you do not want to go."

It's a verse you never really notice until the day you are led there too.

Stories of pain vary in their degree, but at some point they find their way to the same place: *Darkness.* These are some of the words that propel us to that place:

"We found something on your tests."

"We are letting you go."

"I want a divorce."

"I can't marry you anymore."

These phrases descend on us like unwelcome visitors, and we long to send them away. Instead they beckon us to follow, and we don't get to choose whether or not we go. There is evidence, however, that we don't go there alone — and our response to where we are led can make a difference in how our story unfolds.

CHAPTER 2

LIVING
IN THE DARK

When my engagement ended, I found I would look at my friends and want to live their stories instead of my own. I knew they had mortgages they couldn't pay, children who demanded their attention, spouses they couldn't communicate with. But the absence of those things in my life caused envy rather than sympathy. I wanted anyone's story but mine.

When Jesus tells Peter in John 21 that someday he'll be led where he doesn't want to go, the first thing Peter does is point to another disciple and says, "Lord, what about him?"

It was comforting to know I wasn't alone.

C. S. Lewis alludes to this scene from John 21 in his book *The Horse and His Boy* from The Chronicles of Narnia. When the boy, Shasta, encounters Aslan the lion (who is the Christ figure in the series), they have a conversation in which Aslan retraces his presence in Shasta's life. While Aslan is recounting his involvement in Shasta's story, Shasta wants to know why Aslan wounded his friend Aravis, so he asks a question about her. Aslan responds, "Child, I am telling you your story, not hers. I tell no one any story but his own."[1]

When we find ourselves in a place we'd rather not be, we become interested in other people's stories. Sometimes we wish we could live them. But the only story we get to live is our own.

I was forty-five, single, back in my apartment, and contemplating why I had spent the last three years of my life engaged to a man whose ex-wife would suddenly find him attractive enough to marry again. It certainly wasn't the script I had chosen. At the very least, I wished I could have auditioned for a different part. But that's the difference between life and acting. You don't audition for your role in life. You just get to live it. However, your relationship with the Director *can* make a difference in how your script plays out.

You don't audition for your role in life. You just get to live it. However, your relationship with the Director can make a difference in how your script plays out.

Jon and Stacy were pregnant with their first child when they got their news. The son of a minister, Jon had been a Christian most of his life, and he worked for Habitat for Humanity. Stacy worked at Angels Foster Care, an agency that placed babies born to drug-addicted mothers into the arms of loving parents to receive the care and bonding they needed. Jon and Stacy were the poster couple for producing healthy, well-adjusted children who would grow up understanding what faith really means.

However, that wasn't the script for Jon and Stacy's life. Six months into their pregnancy, they were told that their baby's heart wasn't developing. The doctor was pretty sure the baby would die in utero. But miraculously, that baby hung on, and with each month, Jon and Stacy's faith hung on too.

The doctors gave little hope, but the baby (now named Drake) continued to defy all odds, staying alive in the womb until he could be delivered. Hundreds of people knew of Drake's story because his parents blogged his progress—the obstacles, the miracles, and eventually the birth. It looked as if God was overcoming the odds in bringing this baby into the world. It seemed clear he had a plan for this little life.

Drake lived three days. Long enough to be held, baptized, and ushered into God's presence. It seemed like a tragic end to an unfair story. Why would God string Jon and Stacy along, only to have it end this way? If Drake was going to die, why didn't he die right away, saving this couple the turmoil, tears, and financial strain of this little baby's journey? But these weren't the questions that led Jon and Stacy in their journey with Drake. Instead, they let their baby's life and death become whatever God wanted it to be.

It's impossible to measure the impact of Drake's short life. Jon's dad (Drake's grandpa) had gone from being a pastor of a small church to a denominational missionary leader in the Congo. Baptizing little Drake touched him so profoundly that he and Jon began exploring ways to connect people and resources to children who had no access to the health care

Drake had received. Covenant Kids Congo was birthed the year after baby Drake died. Stacy continues her work to this day, placing uncared-for babies into the arms of loving mothers, many of whom are unable to conceive.

Jon and Stacy's love for their own child has given them an empathy toward hurting parents and children that fuels their lives. It would be understandable if this couple lived in resentment toward God, abandoning their faith because it hadn't produced the result they wanted. But they did not.

In a video interview viewed in our church one Easter morning, they said, "We are grateful that God let Drake be born so we could see him, touch him, and be with him for three whole days."

It seemed like a strange story of hope to share on Easter morning. But Drake's life on earth was as long as Jesus stayed in the grave, and it was clear that both of them lived to show that this life on earth, however short or long, is not the end of the story. As Jon and Stacy's interview went viral and played on thousands of computers across the world, stories of pain and heartbreak found their meaning in Drake's story — that death does not have the final word. Jon and Stacy wouldn't have chosen this chapter in the story of their life. It was given to them to live. But how they lived it made all the difference.

A baby lives for three days. A man finds out his wife has cancer. A woman discovers she married a sex abuser. These hardly sound like stories of faith. Yet the way that they were lived made them just that. These stories show that God is able to take the brokenness of our lives and weave together something we could never imagine, if we keep holding on to him.

But this is hard to do when the circumstances of our lives seem to encourage us to let go and try it on our own.

———◆———

Julie got up and pushed her alarm button. It was 5:30 a.m. Limping to the coffeepot, she was keenly aware how much easier she got up twenty-five years earlier. The retirement package she was building sounded sweeter every year.

Julie knew she shouldn't complain. She had her dream job, and she was thankful. Yes, there were sacrifices—marriage at forty-four, no kids. But she was part of the small percentage of people who actually got paid for doing what she loved to do.

In the past five years, besides getting married, her life had taken another turn, as she had embraced the faith that had drastically changed her brother's life. Raised in a family of atheists, she watched her brother's conversion take him from pot-smoking kid to pastor of a church. It took some time, but Julie, too, came to believe, and she now had someone to thank for the blessings in her life.

As Julie walked into her office, she waved to her boss. Julie's boss usually began the day chatting about which new projects they were involved with, which trips were coming up, how her new marriage was going. But today, there was only silence. Finally he got up and walked toward her, wearing an expression she had never seen.

"Julie, today is your last day," he said. "You've got two hours to clear your desk, and Bob will walk you to your car. Thanks for all you've done for us."

She was dizzy, as if she had just been given a drug. Unable to fully process what was happening, she had no choice but to do as she was told. When Julie woke up that morning, she headed to work at the company she had given the best years of her life to, but by 9:00 a.m., Julie was unemployed.

With no schedule and no plan, Julie's life had suddenly become an open slate. There was both fear and freedom for how she would fill it. A job, of course, topped her to-do list. But if she and her husband tightened their belts, they had a little window of time before she had to jump back in.

Julie's church happened to be doing a mission trip to Haiti the month after Julie was let go from her job. She had always felt a tug when mission trips were announced, but the demands of her schedule had never allowed her to consider it. When the pastor told her there was still room on the trip, she had only her own excuses to battle. She took a step of faith, thinking a change of scenery might do her some good.

The week she spent in Haiti exposed her to a poverty she never knew existed. She had heard about it, of course. But now she'd touched it, and the Haitian people's faces were etched in her mind in a way she'd never be able to erase. Gone were her complaints of losing her six-figure job. A roof over her head and food on the table had become reasons enough for her to be grateful. When Julie came back from Haiti, she looked exactly the same. It was what you couldn't see that was different.

In a twist of fate, the loss of her job gave that gift to her.

In my season of pain, I, too, found I saw things differently. As I went about my day, rather than just dealing with people in their "roles" of clerk, waitress, grocery bagger, fellow shopper, I wondered about their stories. I had a new compassion for what each of them might be facing in their lives. *Had any of them just lost a fiancée? A husband? A child? Had the man over in produce just received word that he had six months left to live?*

I also found I was drawn to help people who had bigger stories of pain, maybe as a kind of therapy to gain a new perspective on my own. Eventually I was led to the inner city of Los Angeles, where an organization called "S.A.Y. Yes!" (an acronym for "Save America's Youth") ran an afterschool program at a church right in the heart of Skid Row. I had visited the kids in this program several times as a youth pastor with my students, but during this new season in my life, I went there to volunteer once a week. These innocent, neglected children weren't living on Skid Row because of choices they made; they were there because they were born there — which put my broken engagement into a broader perspective.

Serena* was an eleven-year-old girl whom I met through the program, and I began feeling the nudge (since I wasn't a wife or mother) that I should get more personally involved in her life. I hadn't the slightest idea how I would do that, as we lived in totally different worlds. But I somehow felt connected to her because of my pain.

I asked her if I could come early on my volunteer day to pick her up from school and spend some time with her, and she

---

* Not her real name.

accepted the invitation. The first day we went to her "home," a Skid Row hotel room her father was renting by the month, I couldn't believe it was where she lived. The smell was indescribable—a mixture of dirty clothes, rat droppings, and leftover food sitting next to a Bunsen burner, which served as their stove.

This precious girl grew up in this run-down hotel, as did many of the other children who were a part of the "S.A.Y. Yes!" program. Most of the children lived with their mothers, but because Serena's mom was on the streets, she ended up with her dad.

The more time I spent with Serena and the other children of Skid Row, the more I saw my suffering through a wider lens. Though the pain I experienced from my broken engagement was still very real and raw, this little girl and the other children in the program helped me lift my eyes. In a way, it was a Job-like experience.

If you are unfamiliar with his story, Job was a man who loved God and who was also richly blessed by him. Then God permitted the devil to take those blessings away—one by one. Once rich and happy, surrounded by family, Job was now poor, lonely, and diseased. The only relative he had left was his wife, who comforted him with the words "Curse God and die!"* (Maybe marriage wasn't such a good idea after all.)

But Job hung on to God, in spite of his circumstances and his wife's advice. He cried and wailed and complained and suffered, but he didn't let go. He struggled with God instead of abandoning him.

---

* Job 2:9.

Job's journey through his pain led him to shift his gaze from his own tiny life to the expansive life that God had created. By giving him a sweeping tour of the universe, God showed Job that he was part of a much bigger picture. Job's life was not just about Job.

I didn't get invited (as Job did) to a sweeping tour of the universe to look at whales and hippos and other amazing creatures too big and complex to understand. Instead, I got invited to look at a part of God's world that was located only an hour away in downtown Los Angeles. There he showed me children hidden in a corner of the world I never would have known existed if pain hadn't led me there.

Pain came into my life as an uninvited guest, and after trying to wish it away, I followed it. It turns out God was in the darkness of my pain.

It didn't change my circumstances. But it changed me.

CHAPTER 3

PRAYING FOR ONE THING ... AND GETTING SOMETHING ELSE

Serena was just starting junior high when we began meeting. It was the age most inner-city kids dropped out of school because of lack of parental support. Since God had answered my prayer for children by bringing me this child, I decided he had made it my job to help Serena make it through.

I had prayed for a husband and a child of my own. Instead, God gave me singleness and someone else's child to care for. I was beginning to wonder if God and I spoke different languages.

During my visits to the inner city, for a breath of fresh air I'd occasionally bring Serena home with me, and we'd spend a night together just being girls. Watching her experience things I had in abundance helped me experience them in new ways. Simple things such as family and food. Love and laughter. The pit I had in my stomach for the husband I missed became tempered by gratefulness for what I had.

Serena gave me that gift.

She grew quiet in the car each time I returned her to her home. It was as if she peeled off layers when she came to visit my world and slowly put them back on as she returned to hers. Was it invisible armor? In many ways she *was* a soldier, fighting a battle I'd never know.

> I had prayed for a husband and a child of my own. Instead, God gave me singleness and someone else's child to care for. I was beginning to wonder if God and I spoke different languages.

In spite of her hardships, Serena graduated from junior high. That alone was a major feat, for most kids in her situation dropped out long before. We took a breath and committed to four more years.

Her sophomore year, Serena got pregnant. The amazing thing was, she didn't even *know* she was pregnant. As her belly grew and I began to suspect it wasn't a case of adolescent weight gain, I gently told her it was time to go to the doctor. When she did, she found out she was five months along.

Unlike the girls around her, many of whom became pregnant at that same age, Serena decided her baby deserved a different life. Against the counsel of her father (who had no means of supporting her and was at that time dying of AIDS), Serena made the brave decision to place her baby for adoption. She knew adoption was her baby's ticket to a different life from the one she had.

In the months that followed, Serena and I pored over books of prospective adoptive parents until she finally found the best match. And then, five weeks early, her little boy was born. He was perfect — ten toes, ten fingers, and the spitting image of his beautiful mother. Later that same day, I got a call from the adoption agency.

His prospective parents decided they wanted a girl.

I knew that with this news Serena would change her mind and keep the baby.

I whispered to the air as she slept. "God, is this what you want?" As I gazed at this helpless infant, I knew his whole life hung on the line of this unanswered prayer.

Because Serena had signed the papers for adoption, her baby was taken into temporary foster care. Three days later, I was at my friend's house, pouring out my heart about Serena's baby's plight. Suddenly she said, "I know this couple who's been trying to have a baby for a very long time. I'm not sure if they've thought about adoption, but ..."

I interrupted her. "Should we call them?"

Tom and Linda Bender both worked at Mariners Christian School, and they were loved by all the students. However, it was their deepest yearning to have children of their own. Dozens of families across their community had prayed for the baby who would one day be lucky enough to be born into their home. They couldn't have dreamed how the answer to their prayer was being formed.

We quickly set up a meeting, and with a high five and a *yes*, my sweet fifteen-year-old girl decided this couple was the right choice for her baby boy. Less than a week later, Serena and I delivered her nine-day-old child to Tom and Linda. There were no adoption papers yet, no agency involved. A lawyer was called, the baby stayed, and within a month the adoption was complete.

Tommy Jr. had found his home, and Serena served as the channel through which God delivered him.

After Serena gave birth to Tommy, she continued going to school. Her dad died of AIDS during her junior year. Two women from the "S.A.Y. Yes!" program volunteered to let Serena stay with them so she could finish high school—and between the three of us, we helped her make it through.

One year later, after traversing what seemed to be a gigantic mound of term papers and challenges, Serena graduated in 2003. As I watched my girl literally dance across the stage to receive her diploma, tears filled my eyes. Thousands of kids walked across the stage that day in high schools all over the country, but somehow I knew heaven was applauding in a special way just for Serena.

If God had answered my earlier prayer, I wouldn't have been there to see it.

———————

In 2 Corinthians 12, Paul prays three times for God to remove a "thorn" from his life. We don't know what Paul's thorn was; we only know that God didn't remove it. For Paul, it was an unanswered prayer.

There are people who don't want to get married, and for them, singleness is not a thorn. But singleness was my thorn, and I prayed fervently that God would take it away. Whatever Paul's thorn was, the Bible says that instead of taking it away, God gave him the tools to live with it: "My grace is sufficient for you, for my power is made perfect in weakness" (2 Corinthians 12:9).

But I didn't pray for power; I prayed for thorn removal.

That may have been my response but it wasn't Paul's. Instead, Paul took God's non-answer to his prayer as his answer. Rather than continuing to focus on his thorn, he changed his trajectory.

> Therefore I will boast all the more gladly about my weaknesses, so that Christ's power may rest on me. That is why, for Christ's sake, I delight in weaknesses, in insults, in hardships, in persecutions, in difficulties. For when I am weak, then I am strong.
>
> 2 CORINTHIANS 12:9–10

This verse has been quoted thousands of times and has inspired millions of lives. Maybe part of why Paul went through this trial was so he could write it. Paul accepted God's answer and moved on in his faith. But I have to wonder, did he keep praying about that thorn?

I can tell you I did. All the way through my relationship with Serena, I prayed that God would bring me a husband. The pain I went through paled in comparison to what she faced in her day-to-day life, but she understood it. Whether you are rich or poor, raised in a Skid Row hotel or a suburban home, companionship is a universal desire. And she grieved that it eluded me. However, looking back, my disappointment may have been the best gift I could have given her.

Serena needed a God who was not just equated with blessings. She needed a God who could walk with her in her pain. She watched as God did that with me. For a girl who had been raised on Skid Row, faith in the midst of disappointment was just the faith she needed to find.

The cycle of the inner city was one I came to know well, and it took a miracle for someone to break out. Serena came so close to being that miracle—graduating from high school and even going on to college. We raised money, got her a scholarship, and rallied her on. I attended college freshman orientation with her, full of hope for her future.

But the years of her upbringing took an understandable toll on Serena's ability to succeed. As her grades dropped and her attendance waned, I knew she was losing the battle. I drove to the university to try to encourage her, and we sat together in silence at a Jack in the Box restaurant up the street. As I studied her countenance, a thin shell seemed to have formed since I had seen her last.

As we talked, she looked down at her chicken sandwich, her face hollow and expressionless. When I finished my attempts to cheer her on, the pools in her eyes released a single tear, which slowly rolled down her cheek. Her expression remained unchanged.

Serena left the university at the end of the year. I told her that her decision was more than okay, that college wasn't for everybody. But her disappointment in herself disconnected her from everyone in her life who had rallied her on.

Eventually we lost touch. She moved from one friend's place to another, and then she stopped returning my calls. Some time later, I found out through others that she had two more kids. A year ago, she became my friend on Facebook.

Serena's firstborn boy, now ten, continues to thrive. He

has two brothers, each with miracle stories of their own and neither of whom is biological to Tom and Linda.

Perhaps grown son will one day find his biological mother. Perhaps biological mother will one day be inspired by her grown son. But no matter what happens, I watched my involvement in Serena's life change the course of history for one boy, and that was reason enough for me to be a part of it.

When God doesn't answer our prayers in the direction we wish, we can dwell in the disappointment of what isn't — or we can ask for what we need in the reality of what is. It comes down to perspective.

Not having children of my own created space in my life I neither asked for nor wanted. But it was that space that led me to Serena. Through our relationship, I discovered that you don't have to be married to have a child. There are children all over the world for us to have. They live in inner cities and Third World countries, and they pray every day for people to come into their lives.

C. S. Lewis reflects in an essay on prayer that perhaps the strongest and bravest are not the ones who "name it and claim it" but the ones who are willing to give up their claim, even if it's just for a time, to participate in a greater battle.[2]

I'm ashamed to admit I didn't want to participate in that battle. But God brought it to me by keeping what I did want away. Looking back, I am grateful. Sometimes God withholds what we want so he can give us what others

> *Sometimes God withholds what we want so he can give us what others need. And we are the better for it. Our lives become bigger than just us.*

need. And we are the better for it. Our lives become bigger than just us.

Without a doubt, Jesus Christ modeled this most eloquently. Knowing the excruciating journey to the cross that lay ahead, he cries out in Gethsemane, "Father, if you are willing, take this cup from me." His prayer is met with silence. His response to the silence is his prayer: "Yet not my will, but yours be done" (Luke 22:42).

Jesus accepted God's no so the world could experience God's yes. Could he have done this partly so we would follow his lead?

With so many pointing to answered prayer as a sign of God's favor, it may seem strange to say that unanswered prayer could be a sign of greater favor still. Yet the evidence is there.

Using Jesus as an example, Lewis wrote, "He who served Him best of all said, near His tortured death, 'Why hast thou forsaken me?' When God becomes man, *that Man, of all others, was least comforted by God, at His greatest need.*"[3]

Because of this staggering truth, Lewis pushes against equating answered prayer with God's favor. Instead he goes on to reflect:

If we were stronger, we might be less tenderly treated.
If we were braver, we might be sent, with far less help,
to defend far more desperate posts in the great battle.

Maybe our unanswered prayers can be viewed as God's greatest answers, for they leave room for us to rise up and answer his call.

CHAPTER 4

A WEANED FAITH

Trust, by its very nature, must overcome distance to build its bridge. And yet that distance, when it comes to God, can just as easily produce doubt. This seems to be a risk God is willing to take.

In my season of basking in the silence of God, my eyes caught a short psalm in the Bible I had never noticed before:

> My heart is not proud, LORD,
>   my eyes are not haughty;
> I do not concern myself with great matters
>   or things too wonderful for me.
> But I have calmed and quieted myself,
>   I am like a weaned child with its mother;
>   like a weaned child I am content.
> Israel, put your hope in the LORD
>   both now and forevermore.
>
> PSALM 131

37

I thought about the image of a weaned child, beginning to be taught to feed on his own, and what that process feels like for a child. What that process feels like for a mom. What it would be like if the weaning never happened.

Time magazine ran an article on "attachment parenting" in May 2012, which included a cover shot of a mom dressed in workout clothes, breastfeeding her three-year-old boy. The child was standing on a chair, while his mother stood next to him and nursed him. If it was going for shock value, *Time* succeeded, and I'm sure there were more than a few discussions around the watercooler concerning the "right" time to wean a child.

From my own point of view, it seems the more articulately a child can ask for a breast, the more likely it is time for the mother to withhold it. (The whole teeth thing is another conversation altogether.) Nevertheless, no matter what we believe about when to wean a child, I have never witnessed an adult breastfeeding. So I conclude that at one time or another, we have all been withheld from something we want by someone who loves us—which may be one way to understand how it works with God.

What does it look like when God weans us? Maybe more importantly, what does it feel like? When we feel God withholding, pulling back, or staying silent, we are tempted to cry out, *"You don't love me!"* In fact, just the opposite may be true.

After my engagement broke off, I would wake from a blissful sleep and lie there looking at the ceiling, whispering a halfhearted prayer. *"Why have you done this to me?"* I felt abandoned, uncared for, and alone. It never really occurred to me to think about what God was feeling.

When a mother withholds something from her child, it pains

her when her child believes she doesn't love him. But because she does love her child, her greatest desire is that he grows. And so she is willing to deny her child and sacrifice his temporary affection for the growth he'll experience for his future.

Could this be a microcosm of how God feels about us?

Author Philip Yancey says there are three questions we struggle with when we feel God's distance and want or need him to be close. The questions are these: *Why is God hidden? Why is God silent? Why is God unfair?* At the root of our doubts, usually one of these three questions lurks.

As our souls are weaned, we are sometimes permitted to live in these questions for months and years at a time. Some handle it by embracing a lukewarm faith, relegating God to the category of Santa Claus or the Tooth Fairy. You don't want to give him up altogether, but you no longer expect anything from him. However, you still visit him on holidays and in times of need.

Others divorce him altogether.

And then there is a third choice, described in Jon and Stacy's story, as well as the stories of many others. It's the willingness to live in the disappointment and silence, waiting to see how God shows up. It may not happen the way we think it should or want it to, but it may be our first glimpse of the God who truly is.

———— ◦▸◂◦ ————

All Shannon had ever wanted to be was a mom, and when she fell in love with Dave, she found someone who mirrored her parental yearnings. Parenthood was a longing each of them felt, and their desire doubled in intensity when they became husband and wife.

After they went through six years of trying to get pregnant, the doctor gave them the hopeful news that they could have a baby at any time. He could find nothing wrong with either of them. The problem was, they *weren't* having a baby, and as they watched rounded bellies and car seats spring up all around them, the hole in their hearts grew. After thousands of unanswered prayers, Shannon and Dave quietly sat in the silence of God.

Then, one day in church, a young woman stepped onto the stage to make an announcement. The woman worked for Angels Foster Care, an organization Shannon had heard about a few other times. As this woman talked about babies born in desperate situations, Shannon felt God break his silence. This wasn't the path she had prayed for, but a strange stirring told her this was the answer to her prayer. Dave's response confirmed her feelings.

God had surfaced—not in the way they expected or hoped for, but in a way neither of them could ignore. As this dear couple went through the battery of tests required to become foster parents, their longings were reshaped and changed. They would no longer focus their efforts solely on delivering a child; instead they became available for a child to be delivered to their home.

When little Miss Ruby came to Angels, she was loved by everyone she met. You couldn't just call her Ruby; she was "Miss Ruby" to everyone who crossed her path. With her diminutive stature and porcelain-doll looks, she housed a personality double her size. No one could resist her, though she had been caught in a whirlwind of unforeseen circumstances that had kept her from being permanently placed. Because Ruby was older than most Angels babies, the selection of her next family was careful and deliberate. At this point, Ruby needed more than temporary foster housing; what she needed was a permanent home.

With a swift phone call from the Angels social worker, Shannon and Dave became that home. Skipping the experience of potty training and guiding first steps, they became "Mommy and Daddy" the minute that Ruby walked into their lives. In the months that followed, Ruby helped her parents become those names, though she started calling them that the day they met. Because Shannon and Dave were willing to widen their lens for the answer to their prayer, they also became the answer to another prayer. And when Ruby was permanently adopted into their family, they never doubted for a minute that she was meant to be theirs.

———————

The silence of God is temporary, usually for the purpose of doing more than we ask. However, it almost always involves loss. One of the ways we survive our loss is by looking outside of our own experience to find hope. As the social worker who delivered Ruby watched this family come together, she couldn't help but feel it had been orchestrated by God. And this was one of the places she returned to look for God when her three-day-old baby Drake was taken.

The stories of our lives are big stories, full of heartbreak and hope. They are connected in ways we never imagine, and sometimes never see. Trust is the willingness to put the "great matters" of Psalm 131 into God's hands, knowing we will never really understand the big picture of all that's going on. However, we can get a greater glimpse of God's work when we are willing to look beyond our own stories and let God meet us in the stories of others.

Yancey makes the point that the root of these questions— *Why is God silent? Why is God hidden? Why is God unfair?*—is inevitably personal. "We're really asking, Why is God unfair *to me*? Why does he seem silent *with me*, and hidden *from me*?"[4] This seems to me to be an important distinction when it comes to finding our faith in the dark.

> God might not be doing what we want him to do, but that doesn't necessarily make him any less God. We just may have to broaden our focus in order to see him.

God might not be doing what *we* want him to do, but that doesn't necessarily make him any less God. We just may have to broaden our focus in order to see him. It was Stacy who brought God's path of hope to Shannon and Dave. Shannon and Dave in turn brought God's hope back to Stacy. Neither couple got what they had asked for, but both were changed by what they got. In the process, their faith was weaned.

Why does God want us to have faith in him apart from what he gives us? Maybe because it's the only way to win our love. When we love someone for what they give us, our devotion is reduced to passion for the things that we get. The Giver becomes trumped by the allure of his gifts.

God wants more than our conditional allegiance, and he's willing to risk it for the sake of our love. Douglas John Hall writes, "God's problem is not that God is not able to do certain things. God's problem is that God loves! Love complicates the life of God as it complicates every life."[5]

Perhaps it's this quest for love that keeps God from morphing himself into a Santa Claus figure, satisfied purely in the joy of answering our requests. It appears God wants more, and in his gamble to pursue us wholly, he takes the risk of losing us altogether. Like a wise suitor, he knows it's all or nothing in the quest for the human heart.

Before calamity hits Job, we are privy to a conversation between Satan and God that Job knows nothing about. Satan has been roaming the earth, presumably in search of someone to tempt, and it is God who initiates the dialogue. Like a proud parent getting out pictures of his kids, God says, "Have you considered my servant Job? There is no one on earth like him; he is blameless and upright, a man who fears God and shuns evil" (Job 1:8).

God's tone comes close to bragging, as if he was "showing off" his greatest child. But Satan, true to form, throws a crimp in God's affirmation: "Of course he loves you! Who wouldn't with all the stuff you've given him? Take it away, and he will curse you—I guarantee it" (loose paraphrase of Job 1:9–11, Laurie Short).

Let's pause here for a minute and try to put ourselves in the mind of God. What are his choices? One is to walk away, essentially exposing his doubt that Job might not be the man he has just told Satan he is. The other is to accept Satan's challenge, putting his prized child in harm's way and opening himself to the possibility that Job will do exactly what Satan predicts.

This is a big scene for the journey of our faith, and I think a profound one for getting at the heart of God. We discover from this dialogue that it is out of God's affirmation, not his punishment, that Job's descent into pain is approved.

God accepts Satan's experiment. The drama unfolds, and one by one, Job's provisions, family, and health are all taken away. Job's wife does exactly what Satan expects. Remarkably, however, Job does not, beginning his journey into pain with amazing compliance. When confronted by his wife he says, "Shall we accept good from God, and not trouble?" (Job 2:10).

I wonder what must have welled up in God's heart when he heard those words.

Job *is* eventually provoked to anger, though not by his circumstances. His irritation is aroused by his "friends," who insist, due to the limitations of their theology, that Job must have done something to deserve this terrible fate. Only then do we hear Job cry out in protest, proclaiming an innocence that we (as the audience) already know.

The book goes on to describe some of the great questions of the faith regarding suffering; however, the book ends with no more answers about pain than when it begins. Nevertheless, it is *in* Job that we see God's work. God's gamble is ultimately rewarded, as Job is able to separate his faith from his circumstances. Through his trial, Job's faith has been weaned.

In losing all that God had given him, Job gained a better understanding of God. As a result, his devotion deepened. Perhaps Job himself did not know what he would do if God withheld everything from him — but at the end of his journey he does. Therefore, it seems the end result was primarily not about Job's circumstances. It was about Job.

The book of Job is silent about God's feelings during Job's calamity, but we are given a small peek into God's heart when he puts a restraint on Satan's request. Twice he tells Satan that he must spare Job's life, and it is evident from the opening scene that God does not instigate Job's pain, but is, in fact, Job's cheerleader through it. God is on Job's side, not Satan's. Nevertheless, the great mystery remains that in his farsightedness, God has made allowance for pain. What Job couldn't know is what we now know in Jesus — that God also endures it on our behalf.

Right after God takes Job on a sweeping tour of the universe, Job is no less diseased or broken than when his tour began. And yet Job is healed by discovering the sheer size of God. In the last chapter of the book, he ends his cries with this surrender:

> "I know that you can do all things;
>   no purpose of yours can be thwarted.
> You asked, 'Who is this that obscures my plans
>   without knowledge?'
> Surely I spoke of things I did not understand,
>   things too wonderful for me to know."
>
> JOB 42:2–3

You can almost hear Psalm 131 echo in Job's words. Then Job goes on: "You said, 'Listen now, and I will speak; I will question you, and you shall answer me.' My ears had heard of you but now my eyes have seen you. Therefore I despise myself and repent in dust and ashes."

The irony of Job repenting, after all the suffering God has allowed in his life, shows that a huge shift has happened in his perspective. No longer is Job caught up in "*why?*" Instead, Job is overwhelmed with "*who?*" It seems his questions no longer need answers for him to have confidence in God.

Job eventually gains back double what he had before. And yet his losses remain. New children replace old ones, but they don't resolve Job's grief. However, at the end of the book, the real story is not about what Job gained or lost but about what happened inside of him.

Job trusts, and that, it seems, was the point of his journey.

Part II

GOD IN
THE DARK

God holds back; he hides himself; he weeps. Why?
Because he desires what power can never win. He is
a king who wants not subservience, but love.

—Philip Yancey, *Disappointment with God*

CHAPTER 5

HIGHER THOUGHTS

Imagine if God had allowed Job to glimpse the cosmic battle that swirled in the heavens above him — if Job had been given the knowledge he was participating in a script much bigger than his own. Suppose the sky had been peeled back and Job could have seen, just for a moment, how significant he was in a story he knew nothing about.

Of course, this would have changed Job's journey altogether, because it was his *inability* to see that made the story what it was. In the end, God did give Job a glimpse of the bigger picture, giving Job a clue that God was directing a stage much broader than his own.

The prophet Isaiah paints a picture of the partnership between us and God, bringing into view the broader scope of God's perspective:

> "For my thoughts are not your thoughts,
>   neither are your ways my ways,"
>   declares the LORD.

"As the heavens are higher than the earth,
 so are my ways higher than your ways
 and my thoughts than your thoughts."

ISAIAH 55:8–9

Job understood this, at least in part, after he glimpsed the world through God's spectacles. However, Job's story was lived within the limits of his own view. This is how all stories are lived.

In 1998, Jim Carrey starred in a movie called *The Truman Show*, which was about a man who lived his entire life on the set of a reality TV show, except for one important distinction—he never knew his life was being filmed. Everyone else knew they were part of a cast, but for Truman, the show *was* his reality. The director made sure Truman never saw life outside the city, which was his set.

Then one day, by accident, a stage light drops from the sky, landing at Truman's feet. He is stunned. From this point on, Truman begins to piece together clues that there might be a bigger reality than he is able to see. We as the audience see what Truman cannot, and we root for him to discover the world beyond the set so he can be free. However, we sense that it might not be best for Truman to have the sky opened all at once. This could overwhelm him and send him further back into the safety and ignorance of his two-dimensional life.

The director of Truman's show, much like Satan in Job's story, is invested in confining Truman to his limited perspective. Thus he creates obstacles to keep Truman from breaking through to the other side—artificial fires and storms to keep him trapped inside the city. The closer Truman gets to his freedom, the harder his journey becomes. The process of "leaving the set" becomes Truman's great quest, and we cheer him on as he endures the obstacles to discover the truth of who he really is.

Perhaps this is a small picture of our own journey of faith. With God as our audience, we live our lives within the limits of our perspective. However, many of us have a sense that there is more going on than we can see. When we witness a baby's birth, gaze at a sunset, or peek into a microscope or telescope, we have an inkling of a greater reality. But the bulk of our lives are lived within the "set" of our immediate experience.

Like a stage light dropping from the sky, God sends us clues that there is more going on than we can see. However, he refrains from opening the whole sky. Perhaps this would overwhelm us. Certainly it would eliminate our need for faith. Frederick Buechner reflects, "Without somehow destroying me in the process, how could God reveal himself in a way that would leave no room for doubt? If there were no room for doubt, there would be no room for me."[6] God makes room for our faith, and in so doing, he makes room for our doubts.

> God makes room for our faith, and in so doing, he makes room for our doubts.

However, there may be another reason God refrains from full disclosure. He could be protecting us by not "paring back the sky" because our senses just couldn't handle it. Truman's exposure to the reality of another world had to come slowly and deliberately; otherwise his two-dimensional mind would not have been able to grasp it. Maybe God knows the same is true for us.

Philip Yancey describes the dilemma God may feel by imagining what it would be like to communicate with a creature on a microscope slide. For the creature, "the universe" consists of only two dimensions, so from our three-dimensional vantage point, we see a world this creature wouldn't be able to comprehend. In a similar way, the unseen world exists outside our range of perception, and it is only through rare interventions—dropping stage lights, so to speak—that we are awakened to the possibility of the other side. Perhaps the only way God can communicate the reality of his universe is by giving us a small peek into the expanse of his world. Because we exist on a plane so far below him, we cannot comprehend the total picture with our present faculties.[7]

The analogy of being compared to a creature on a microscope slide fits for me when I read the book of Revelation, for there I am aware that the reality of another world is locked in a language I do not yet know. The images in this book paint a picture of a spiritual world that is beyond my comprehension. And yet, I am able to grasp small glimpses of its reality within the realm of my experience.

Perhaps you've had those glimpses too.

Like Truman, these glimpses give us hints that we are destined to become more than we are, and that we exist in a world that is bigger than the one we see. Why else would we have the ability to step outside our lives and make observations about our human experience?

C. S. Lewis notes that when we say, "How he's grown!"

or "How time flies!" it is as strange as a fish being repeatedly surprised at the wetness of water — "unless of course the fish were destined to become, one day, a land animal."[8] Could our reflections hint at what we will one day become?

Certainly, there are many clues that God set eternity in our hearts. Poets, philosophers, and artists speak to us in a language that awakens something bigger inside. And yet the fact remains that we exist within the time and space of our present circumstances.

Because of our limited faculties, we are left with only hints that there may be more going on than we can see. For some, these clues are not compelling enough to explore. For others, they lead to a lifelong journey of faith. I have continually been struck throughout my life by how some people are able to live comfortably without pondering the question of what lies beyond.

For reasons I don't completely understand, I have always pondered. From the time I looked up to the sky as a little girl and saw light peering down from the clouds in the shape of a spotlight, I have always felt the experience of "being watched." In time, my ponderings led to a search for God, and I eventually embraced the God of the Christian faith. In a world I found to be increasingly riddled with pain, a God who came to suffer and die and overcome that pain was the only God that made sense to me.

The question that understandably keeps many people from embracing a faith is this: *Where is God when it hurts?* In the cross of Jesus Christ, we find an answer to that question. In his resurrection, we find hope beyond it.

Nevertheless, there are many who choose not to explore the deeper questions of where and who God is. Our life experiences can encourage or discourage a need or desire to seek God. Ironically, I have observed that it is pain rather than joy that is most likely to compel someone toward a journey into faith. Perhaps this is because pain alerts us to a condition we don't have the power to fix.

C. S. Lewis states simply, "God whispers to us in our pleasure ... but shouts in our pains."[9] Certainly Job found this to be true. As his journey descended further and further into pain, he became increasingly less distracted to think of anything else *but* God. For this reason, pain can be a door, rather than a wall, into discovering a reality beyond.

———— ✦ ————

As new parents, Shannon and Dave settled into a new chapter of life with little Miss Ruby, and they couldn't help talking about the way God had worked in their suffering and loss. One night, at a dinner for young couples, they were introduced to Jen and Adam, who were in the throes of trying to start a family. As Shannon and Dave told their story, Jen felt a knot in her stomach grow.

Once alone, Jen turned to Adam and said, "I can't believe they were so happy about adopting." Adam sat in silence, stifling the fact that he had already contemplated that course. This would not be *their* route, Jen thought to herself. They were going to *have* their babies. Maybe it hadn't happened yet, but it was only a matter of time.

As days and weeks turned to months and a year, Jen and Adam began to accept the fact that their "route" might not be what they planned. They were in a church small group with Jon and Stacy, and one day Jen could fight the internal nudge no longer. She met with Stacy to find out more about Angels Foster Care, and Stacy told her of the need for more families. Halfway hoping they would not be selected, Jen and Adam signed up. At the very least, foster care would be "good practice" for the baby they still hoped they'd have.

It was just before summer, and Jen and Adam had planned a long trip away, renting out their home to cover their cost. Two weeks later, Jen got a phone call—a baby Stacy hadn't expected to survive had grown to three pounds and appeared to be getting stronger each day. Would they be interested in caring for her?

Immediately, Jen thought *no*—but her heart told her the answer was *yes*. The irony of waiting so long to have a baby and getting one so quickly struck her that this might be part of a bigger plan.

Their home was rented, their trip was planned, and their life had been interrupted. However, Jen and Adam were surprised by the joy they both secretly felt. Baby Caylee was put in their care, and the minute they saw her, she became lodged in their hearts. A year and a half later, she was adopted as their own.

As this baby grew and eventually became the pride and joy of their lives, Jen thought back to the dinner they'd had with Shannon and Dave. The sadness and pain she felt at the prospect of not giving birth had thawed into joy and wonder. They felt chosen, and she and Adam would point to that night as the first step God used to lead them on this journey.

———————

God not only shouts to us in our pain; he often shouts to others through it. In some mysterious way, pain moves through our lives to touch others. I am not nearly as moved by testimonies of success as I am by testimonies of loss — particularly when something beautiful emerges from that loss. That seems to me to be the most compelling evidence that God exists.

In the stories woven through this book, I hope to paint a picture of some of the glimpses we get of God, particularly in seasons of pain. When we are in the dark, we long for these glimpses, as they can give us purpose and meaning in our pain. They also give us hope that one day we might see our pain differently — or, at the very least, that we might see the good that our pain produced.

In the dark, we often feel distance from God, which is why we need to widen our gaze to see him. We get so focused on where we want God to be that we sometimes miss where he actually is. Stories help us find him, and sometimes, as Jen and Adam learned, they can even help us find ourselves.

Perhaps that is the first step to breaking through to the other side.

CHAPTER 6

GOD OF THE PRESENT TENSE

If you could peek into the minds of people around you, chances are you'd find very few of them completely absorbed in the moment they are living right now. Some may be replaying a conversation they just had, thinking of all the things they should have said. Others are dreaming about a person they're excited to see, and what outfit they should wear (or buy). A few might be going over a presentation they're about to make, just to be sure they've got it down. And at least half the population is thinking about a sports team, and why in the world they gave away that point.

Our minds meander from the past to the future, with only brief stops in the present. Most of our emotions are tied to something that was or will be — until that rare moment when something demands all our attention, propelling us to live entirely in the now. These can be our most promising moments, for it is in the now that God can be found.

Henri Nouwen writes, "If we could just be, for a few minutes each day, fully where we are, we would indeed discover that we are not alone."[10] When we clear our minds of past and future thoughts, we can be in the moment that is, and this, Nouwen says, is the place where we are most likely to encounter God.

Exodus 3 describes this kind of moment, when an eighty-year-old shepherd named Moses becomes captivated by a burning bush. Puzzled by the fact that the bush continues to flame and not burn, Moses draws near. And when he does, he hears a voice from within the bush call him by name:

> "Moses! Moses!"
> And Moses said, "Here I am."
> "Do not come any closer," God said. "Take off your sandals, for the place where you are standing is holy ground."
>
> EXODUS 3:4–5

With his shoes off and attention rapt, Moses stares at the burning bush. The voice continues: " 'I am the God of your father, the God of Abraham, the God of Isaac and the God of Jacob.' At this, Moses hid his face, because he was afraid to look at God."

All at once, Moses is jolted into the extraordinary. The God he has worshiped, learned about, and believed in is calling his name. It's interesting to note that the voice identifies itself just after Moses is invited to stand in a new way on ground he's been on many times before. The common ground has become holy ground, and from that vantage point, Moses is positioned to hear and see things differently. From this point forward, Moses will never be the same.

These burning-bush moments occur in our lives when we, like Moses, are invited to stand in a new way in our circumstances, fully present in the now. Various triggers can usher us into this place—heightened fear, great joy, stabs of pain. For this reason, each of these emotions, even the negative ones, can be considered gifts, for they call us into the present by demanding our full attention.

Gerald Sittser, a theology professor who documented his process of grieving in a book called *A Grace Disguised*, describes this experience. After his mother, wife, and daughter all died in a crash, Sittser was overcome with three catastrophic losses all at once. Through his process of grieving, he said that over time he came to observe that deep sorrow is good for the soul for one reason—it makes us more alive to the present moment. This, he says is the "disguised grace" of loss and pain. Because we find it impossible to distract ourselves from our grief, we are forced to live more fully in the now. Though the experience is not pleasant, it is at the same time full of promise. We have the possibility of experiencing our lives in a new way, where what we see before us is more than we've seen before.

I described such an event in chapter 2, when my ordinary trip to the grocery store became this kind of moment. I had a sense of being fully alive to the circumstances around me, and people I had passed and never noticed before suddenly became human.

This happened on a grander scale with Drake's grandpa, after he baptized his grandson just before the newborn child died. When he returned to the Congo, he had a heightened awareness of the lack of health care for Congolese children.

As I mentioned, his trip became a burning-bush moment that ultimately led to the development of a child sponsorship program, largely inspired by baby Drake.

When we are catapulted into those moments of being more fully in the now, while nothing around us may change, what's *inside us* creates change. We are invited to exist in a different way in our circumstances and, like Moses, to draw near to hear the voice of God. In so doing, we position ourselves to have our story changed.

As Moses stands barefoot in front of the bush, the voice continues: "I have indeed seen the misery of my people in Egypt. I have heard them crying out because of their slave drivers, and I am concerned about their suffering ... I have seen the way the Egyptians are oppressing them. So now, go. I am sending you to Pharaoh to bring my people the Israelites out of Egypt" (Exodus 3:7, 9–10).

I imagine Moses' thoughts as he listened to these words. Without warning, he shifts from hearing God's answer to becoming God's answer. It's such a subtle transition, and it's impossible to read this account without feeling Moses' surprise. If we had a translation of the Bible that allowed for Moses' responses to God, we might see something like this:

"I have seen the misery of my people." (*Good.*)

"I am concerned about their suffering." (*Even better.*)

"I have seen the way they are being oppressed." (*Finally!*)

"So now, go." (*Wait ...*) "I am sending you." (*What?*)

Moses learns in this encounter with God that being alive to the present opens us to possibilities we never imagined—not all of them comfortable. Sometimes we want to close our eyes after they've been opened, to wish we hadn't seen or heard the voice beckoning us. By being present to God in this moment, Moses is given the opportunity to trade in his small story for a much bigger story. His decision at this bush will determine his course. It's a great illustration of the risk and the excitement of living in the now.

We may wonder why God didn't call Moses when he was in his prime—positioned in the palace of Egypt, a "second son" to Pharaoh himself. Instead, Moses is called to the job of his life after losing his family, his home, and his people, and wandering forty years through the desert as a lowly shepherd. Like many of us after we've been through grief and trauma, Moses had created a new, much smaller life for himself. It wasn't great, but it was comfortable, and he knew what to expect—until now. God has just handed him an invitation to a bigger story with his name on it.

Sittser writes, "It may be that the present contains the secret of the renewal of life we long for, as if, in looking under the surface of this vast sea of nothingness, we may find another world that is teeming with life."[11]

By being present at the burning bush, Moses is given a glimpse of another world and is invited to become a key player in it. If he accepts the invitation, he will begin a brand-new chapter in his life.

———

Four months after Ryan and I broke up, I was sitting in my apartment when I received a phone call from a pastor I hadn't

Lord, Help me to go through this...

spoken to in years. I assumed he had heard about my broken engagement and was calling to see how I was doing. As soon as he spoke, I knew he must be calling about something else.

"I heard you got married."

"No." (*Pregnant pause.*)

"Oh, I'm sorry."

"Thanks."

"Well, I'm not sure if you'd be interested, but we have a new position that's been funded by our church. Our staff was praying about it, and your name came up."

I didn't say no, but I was thinking it. I told him I'd think about it and call him back.

I wasn't looking for a job, but I was sort of looking for a life. However, I wasn't looking to move out of my comfort zone. I had recently gotten back on my feet, and life had become predictable again. I knew where things were, I knew what was expected of me, and I didn't think I could handle change. Yet deep inside, I was craving it.

Moving to an unknown community seemed like a challenge too big for me to accept. I felt weak and vulnerable. Working at a new church would require courage and strength. Yet somehow I couldn't get past his words "our staff was praying about it, and your name came up."

It was a burning-bush moment for me. An opportunity to be a part of another story was calling my name. I didn't think I had it in me, but somehow I had a vague notion that my response to this call would be monumental in how my story would unfold. With that in mind, I called him back. Shortly afterward, I moved into a new community and began a new chapter of life.

To stay where I was, safe and small, sounded at the time like the most nurturing choice. But it also would have kept me from the great joy and answer to prayer that awaited me in this new adventure. Looking back on my decision, it turns out that God's care for me was in the risk.

I take great comfort that the last few verses of Exodus 3 reveal Moses' reluctance to move into the life God presented to him. Transitions are not easy, for they call us to leave what is familiar. Even if our life isn't all that good, we are comfortable in it. What lies before us may have the potential for greater fulfillment, but it will also require great risk. If we have experienced any disappointment in the way God has worked in our life, stepping out feels like a huge gamble.

Moses looks for security before he takes this gamble. However, he finds that God will not give him what he thinks he needs. Moses asks, "Who am I that I should go to Pharaoh and bring the Israelites out of Egypt?"

God replies, "I will be with you. And this will be the sign to you that it is I who have sent you: *When you have brought the people out of Egypt*, you will worship God on this mountain" (Exodus 3:12, emphasis mine).

Signs are supposed to come *before* things happen, not after. But the God of the present is forcing Moses to trust. Just as God is with Moses right now, he promises to be with him in the future. Moses will discover that when he gets there — and not a minute before.

In his last moments at the burning bush, Moses learns a defining truth about God—one he will rely on and experience throughout his life: "Suppose I go to the Israelites and say to them, 'The God of your fathers has sent me to you,' and they ask me, 'What is his name?' Then what shall I tell them?"

"I AM WHO I AM. This is what you are to say to the Israelites: 'I AM has sent me to you.'"

When I first read Exodus 3:14 as a new Christian, I thought it was a typo. It appeared that God's words were in the wrong tense. In the years that fol-

He is the great I AM. When I am living in the past or the future, I am there without him.

lowed, I discovered by experience that this "wrong tense" is where God lives.

He is the great I AM. When I am living in the past or the future, I am there without him. I have tried getting what I need for my future from the God who is in the now, but I have never been successful. My fears for what lies ahead are forced to wait for God to meet them at that time.

Moses ultimately trusts the great I AM and takes him up on his invitation to become part of a bigger story. It becomes the defining decision of his life.

Imagine what might have happened if Moses hadn't gone, hadn't trusted, hadn't risked. All the movies about Moses find their culmination in his final years, when it seemed "too late" for anything of merit to happen. The present-tense God calls Moses to put his hand in his as he leaves the comfort of his small life in the wilderness, and heads back to Egypt to begin the most memorable chapter in his career.

CHAPTER 7

NEVER THE SAME WAY TWICE

When God does not show up the way we expect or hope, we are disappointed. At worst, we lose faith. But the very thing that can cause us to lose faith can and perhaps should have the opposite effect. God's active personal nature makes him a presence we cannot control. The fact that we can't predict just how he will show up only reinforces his deity.

In *Prince Caspian*, the fourth book in the Narnia series, the four children (Lucy, Peter, Edmund, and Susan) fall back into the land of Narnia, only to find it very different than it was before. They go on a quest to restore the kingdom, and their journey is set to culminate in a great battle. There is no sign of Aslan until Lucy catches a glimpse of him quietly lurking within the trees. She is startled by the quietness of his presence; she expected him to come roaring in to meet them like he did before. She runs to Aslan and throws her arms around him, greatly relieved that he has finally come to their rescue.

But Aslan gently tells Lucy that this time things will be

different. The children will have to face the battle themselves. At this, Lucy can't contain her dismay: "'Oh dear, oh dear,' said Lucy. 'And I was so pleased at finding you again. And I thought you'd let me stay. And I thought you'd come roaring in and frighten all the enemies away—like last time. And now everything is going to be horrid.'"[12]

The Aslan Lucy expected is not the Aslan who meets her now, and she is disappointed. But Aslan's response to Lucy gives her, and us, an important insight about the journey of faith: "'It is hard for you, little one,' Aslan said. 'But things never happen the same way twice.'"

Lucy's initial disappointment in Aslan's appearance is common to many of us. Just when we think we have a handle on how God works in our lives, he does something that throws us off. This presents us with a crisis that can, if we let it, widen our concept of him. We move from having a God shaped by our faith to having a faith shaped by our God. This seems an important and necessary process if we are to continue growing in our faith.

> *We move from having a God shaped by our faith to having a faith shaped by our God.*

For Lucy, the crisis she is presented with ends up being a great moment for her faith development. Here is how her scene with Aslan unfolds:

> Lucy buried her head in his mane to hide from his face. But there must have been magic in his mane. She could feel lion-strength going into her. Quite suddenly she sat up.

"I'm sorry, Aslan," she said. "I'm ready now."

"Now you are a lioness," said Aslan. "And now all Narnia will be renewed."

Lucy had longed for the old Aslan, the one who showed up in their last encounter. But it was the new Aslan who helped Lucy discover something within herself she didn't know she had. The strength she exhibits from here on out reveals a new and braver Lucy, which appears to be the reason for Aslan's approach. Instead of being her answer to the battle, Aslan helps her become a part of his answer. He gives her strength so she can do the battle with his help.

There is another difference in this "new Aslan," which Lucy mentions when she firsts sees him. Through Lucy's words, C. S. Lewis gives us another insight about God and faith.

"Aslan," said Lucy. "You're bigger."

"That is because you are older, little one," answered he.

"Not because you are?"

"I am not. But every year you grow, you will find me bigger."[13]

According to Lewis's words through Aslan, the more we grow, the bigger God becomes. With this in mind, it's possible to say that the less we have God figured out, the more we are maturing in our faith. This is very different growth trajectory from developing the kind of faith that hinges on knowing the way God will move and act.

Once, during a prayer session for a friend with terminal

cancer, we were told by the leader that in order for her to be healed, everyone in the room had to believe with all their heart that this would happen. I remember feeling conflicted; even though I desired her healing from the bottom of my heart, I had no idea what God would do. I wondered if my lack of faith would inhibit her healing. Still, I prayed earnestly with the group.

My friend died soon after.

I often wonder what people do with their faith when they believe with unwavering certainty that God will heal, and he does not. I do know and have experienced God's miraculous answers to prayer; however, I have also experienced God answering in different ways than I prayed. As I read through the New Testament, my experience is not unlike people who lived during the time of Jesus.

Jesus clearly had the power to do what people asked of him—and there were times when he did what he was asked to do. However, as I study his encounters with people, there seems to be no pattern to the way Jesus answered requests; no two stories are alike. I can't find a "formula of faith" that is evident in the way Jesus worked. It seems that when Jesus answered requests for healing, he almost always threw in something else. It was the "something else" that turned out to be the main point of the story. Perhaps this is helpful as we reach out to find God in the dark.

In Mark 2, when four friends bring—or perhaps we should say lowered—a paralyzed man in front of Jesus to be healed, Jesus sees the friends' faith and says to the paralytic, "Son, your sins are forgiven."

I imagine this was an awkward moment for the four men who had brought their invalid friend. (*"Your sins are forgiven"?*) I'm quite sure they didn't have this answer in mind when they stepped out in faith. Thankfully, Jesus threw in the physical healing as a bonus. However, it's interesting to note the crowd that witnessed this event walked away talking more about Jesus forgiving the man's sins than about Jesus helping him walk. It was that part of the healing where they saw a glimpse of God. For the Pharisees, it was a glimpse they didn't want to see.

In a completely different story in Mark 5, a synagogue ruler approaches Jesus to ask him to come with him to heal his daughter. Jesus agrees, but then he stops to heal a poor bleeding woman in the crowd along the way. Jesus stays with the woman as she tells her entire story, while the ruler watches his margin of time slip away. You can feel the ruler's anxiety in the unwritten verses. Here was a woman who was used to being shoved into the background, and a ruler who spent his life in the foreground, and in an instant their roles are reversed. Only after that does Jesus answer, presumably in the wrong order, what both of them asked. Even though both requests for healing were met, it was in the way they were met that we see God.

And then we have the healing of the disabled man in John 5. He had been an invalid for thirty-eight years. When Jesus finds him, he is lying by a pool that people believed held mystical healing powers whenever it was stirred. However, when Jesus asks him if he wants to get well, the man does not say yes. Instead he goes through a litany of excuses for why he *hasn't* gotten well—none of them his fault. Jesus interrupts him and says, "Get up! Pick up your mat and walk."

At once the man is cured, not as a result of his faith, but in spite of it. You are left feeling Jesus' primary agenda was to confront the man's unwillingness to participate in his healing rather than to bring about the healing itself. This is yet another glimpse of the way God works.

In each of these stories, the physical healing is accompanied by something else, which seems to be the bigger point of the story. It is the "something else" in each story that reveals the way God works. We also see in these stories that Jesus mirrors God's nature in not doing what people expect. He does what people need—even when they don't know they need it.

Throughout the New Testament, Jesus' approach to each request was different and unique. Sometimes he healed as a result of a person's faith. Other times he healed as a result of someone else's faith. Occasionally, he healed when there was no faith. Together, his responses prevent us from coming up with a formula of faith when it comes to answered prayer. Through Jesus, we can see that God does answer prayer—but he never seems to do it the same way twice.

The unexpected way in which God shows up surfaces throughout the Old Testament too. For Noah, God showed up through a great and mighty flood. For Abraham, it was a long-awaited promise. For Joseph, it was the fulfillment of a dream. For Hannah, it was the birth of a son. The manifestations of God in the Old Testament are all different—each one unique. People encountered God in a way that was personal to them. But there is no figure in the Old Testament who experiences such a wide variety of manifestations of God as the prophet Elijah. His story bears witness to the fact that God can move and act in many different ways.

When we first meet Elijah in 1 Kings 17, he is told to retreat by himself to a ravine, where God has ordered ravens to feed him. Other Old Testament prophets were called to immediately go to the king and proclaim (or act out) the words God wanted to say. Elijah's instruction, however, is not to *go*, but to *leave*. Verse 6 describes how he received his meals when did what he was told: "The ravens brought him bread and meat in the morning and bread and meat in the evening."

Maybe it's just me, but I would have loved to be a fly on the wall to see that. However, this amazing manifestation was purely for Elijah's benefit. After spending some time with these birds, the word of the Lord comes to Elijah again: "Go at once to Zarephath in the region of Sidon and stay there. I have directed a widow there to supply you with food."

From ravens to a widow. (At least he was going to interact with a human this time.) However, when he gets there, the widow tells him she is about to prepare her last meal and then die because she has no food left. She's not what you would call an optimist. Thankfully, Elijah is fresh off the daily banquet he received from some wild birds, and he proclaims with confidence that God will take care of them. The second way God shows up is that he does just that. The widow takes Elijah at his word and bakes her last loaf of bread, and the oil and flour are miraculously replenished. They continue to be replenished throughout Elijah's stay.

Nearly three years later, the word of the Lord comes to

Elijah with some direction a prophet might "typically" expect: "Go and present yourself to Ahab, and I will send rain on the land" (1 Kings 18:1).

After Elijah presents himself to King Ahab, he bears witness to one of the most powerful manifestations of God recorded in the Old Testament. But this comes after two seemingly insignificant manifestations of God that took almost three years of Elijah's life. As you read on, you can see that they are all strangely related.

Elijah tells Ahab to gather all four hundred and fifty prophets of Baal so that he can challenge them to "a war of the gods." The prophets go first and spend all day dancing before the altar and slashing themselves, frantically trying to summon their god. Verse 29 gives the stark summary of what happened: "But there was no response, no one answered, no one paid attention."

Finally it's Elijah's turn. He douses the altar with water three times and then ushers forth a simple prayer: "LORD, the God of Abraham, Isaac and Israel, let it be known today that you are God in Israel ... Answer me, LORD, answer me, so these people will know that you, LORD, are God, and that you are turning their hearts back again."

Within seconds, the fire of the Lord consumes the altar, even licking up the water in the trench for dramatic effect. As a result, it inspires everyone there, including the prophets of Baal, to shout, "The LORD — he is God! The LORD — he is God!"

It was a moment unlike any other. But it was preceded by puzzling moments similar to what you and I experience in our lives. (Except maybe getting food delivered by ravens.) Nevertheless, it's safe to say that during the first few years of his relationship with God, Elijah experienced the doubt and confusion many of us face in our spiritual journey, especially when we deal with dark seasons. However, looking through a wider lens, we can see God's purpose for them. The faith that God grew in Elijah through a widow and some birds was the faith that empowered Elijah's confidence that fateful day.

Personally, I am glad Elijah's story does not end with a great fiery scene as the final manifestation of God's presence in his life. Otherwise his story might feel like a superhero comic strip. I need this last episode that the Bible includes for my faith.

After Elijah finishes with the prophets of Baal, he grows depressed because he is marked for death by the king and queen. After retreating to a cave to rest and get perspective, he meets God again, and this time it is very different from his previous experience. He witnesses a mighty wind, then a powerful earthquake, and finally a great fire. But 1 Kings 19 says "the LORD was not in the wind ... the earthquake ... the fire." Then Elijah hears a gentle whisper. It is in the whisper that he meets God.

Through Elijah's story, we gain insight about how to notice God's presence, which can be helpful when we are walking in the dark. God shows up in ways we don't expect but in retrospect most need. Rarely does he show up with big, dramatic flair; more often, he shows up in small, unexpected ways. Usually it's personal. Occasionally it's in the company of others.

And it's probably never going to be the same way twice.

CHAPTER 8

MIDDLE
OF THE STORY

All great stories have a moment in them when things look very bad. Ironically, it's the bad that makes the story so good. When the hero faces an insurmountable challenge and somehow triumphs at the end, our hearts soar. And we can't always predict how the triumph will occur. Sometimes it's a great turnaround, sometimes a narrow escape. Other times it's a courageous death. But all great stories have one thing in common—you have to stay with them to the end. If you close the book or walk out of the film too early, you could be left with a very different perspective of the story.

Most of us love good stories. We find it more difficult to *live* a good story. Maybe it's because we forget that the chapters we are living are part of a greater whole. We may recognize that we do not fully understand the events of our lives until we look back, but is it possible to let that perspective reshape the way we live them? Certainly this would help us grow in our faith.

There is an ancient, well-known Chinese fable that illustrates what it would be like if we understood our lives from this perspective. The story goes something like this:

There was an old man who had a beautiful horse. This horse was not only his family's pride and joy; it was also a means to an income for the family. One day, the horse ran away. Fellow villagers visited the

Most of us love good stories. We find it more difficult to live a good story.

old man to offer their condolences for such a stroke of bad luck.

"It could be good; it could be bad. Who can tell?" replied the old man. "It is as it is. My horse is gone."

Perplexed at the man's nonchalance, the villagers went about their business. A few days later, the horse returned with a pack of twelve wild horses in tow. Again the villagers gathered, this time to offer their congratulations at such a stroke of good luck. Now he had twelve more horses with which to make twelve times the income!

"What a godsend!" they said.

"It could be good; it could be bad. Who can tell?" replied the old man again. "All I see is that twelve more horses have appeared."

The next week, while breaking in one of the wild horses, the old man's son fell and broke both of his legs.

"What bad luck!" the villagers exclaimed. "Your son has broken both of his legs. That's terrible. How will you get your work done? You are too old to do it yourself."

"It could be good; it could be bad: Who can tell?" the old man answered in his predictable and frustrating way. "My son has broken his legs. That is all I know."

Shortly thereafter, the government forcibly removed all the able-bodied men from the village, as the country had gone to war. The old man's son, however, was spared since his legs were broken. The wisdom of the man's words was clearly visible — as what seemed to be bad was, of course, very good.

Only time could tell.*

I wish I could have had the wisdom of that old man during the times I've experienced loss, for it would have helped me make room for the way God was working in my life. It was only through living more of my story that I discovered the truth of the old man's words. For whatever reason, when we are struck with calamity, real or apparent, we have an ominous sense that we have somehow come to our end. We summarize our lives in light of these catastrophic events, and feel as though we will fade away into nothingness.

... And then we wake up the next day. That, in and of itself, should create a sense of hope, although for many of us it doesn't feel hopeful. We see it as simply a new day to figure out how to fill. But our perspective on our story can actually shape the way we live it.

This is illustrated in the classic story *Les Misérables* through the life of the protagonist, Jean Valjean. At the beginning of

---

* This story is found on the Internet in dozens of different variations

the story, Valjean has just been released after serving an unjust nineteen-year prison sentence. He is an older, bitter man with a newly open slate. After numerous rejections for employment, he is invited into a priest's home, where he devours the food set before him and plots to steal the priest's silver. With a bag full of stolen goods, Jean Valjean disappears into the night, only to be caught by the French police. He is handcuffed, and forced to return what he had taken. To everyone's amazement, including Jean Valjean's, the priest tells the authorities that the silver was a gift, and that Valjean had, in fact, forgotten to take the candlesticks, which were the most valuable part of his collection. With this amazing stroke of grace, Jean Valjean is set free.

Again he has a newly open slate to fill, but this time his perspective has changed, impacting every circumstance and decision he'll make from here on out.

Jean Valjean continues to be faced with tragedy and loss right up to the end of his life—but he is a different man. He faces his circumstances with strength and stands in the face of despair with shining hope. We are left at the end of the story realizing our life is bigger than our individual life, and it infuses us with courage to live our story well.

I sometimes wonder how our lives would change if we saw them from a wider perspective—if we knew our courage could inspire others the way great pieces of literature inspire us. Being involved in the stories of Jon and Stacy, Shannon and Dave, and Ken and Kim, I became keenly aware that a spotlight shines on our faith in times of loss. Perhaps it's because no one wonders how to live through joy.

During my own season of disappointment, I was making

a living as a Christian speaker, which gave my loss a public platform I would never have chosen. I realized I had to figure out how to tell my story in a way that didn't depress people. I knew I couldn't end my talk with, "Look what God didn't do!" (That would have been one way off the speaking circuit.) The deeper question I had to wrestle with was whether or not I could hold on to my faith in the midst of my disappointment. I knew I couldn't inspire others to have something I wasn't sure I had myself.

Ultimately I was able to reaffirm my faith in the story of Joseph — not the husband-of-Mary Joseph, but rather the one who takes up ten chapters of Genesis. Perhaps because we are given a full account of his story, his life gave me the perspective I needed to go on. Through Joseph I was able to see that I wasn't at the end of my story. As long as my heart was beating, I was still in the middle of it. That made all the difference in the way I viewed my faith.

As the curtain comes up in Genesis 37, Joseph is anything but a hero. He is a cocky, spoiled teenage boy. Clothed in his father's prized robe, he announces to his brothers that he had a dream where his sheaf rose higher than their sheaves and his star rose higher than their stars. Naturally the brothers are less than enthusiastic. Fed up with Joseph's entitled attitude, they plot to kill him, then soften and decide to sell him into slavery instead.

Genesis 39 finds Joseph downgraded from prized son to

purchased slave, belonging to an Egyptian named Potiphar. However, it is here in the story that Joseph begins to shine. Instead of becoming bitter, he makes the best of his new and not-so-desirable circumstances, and Potiphar rewards him by putting him in charge of his entire household. Much to Joseph's chagrin, Potiphar's wife decides she would like to be included in the gift. After repeated sexual advances, she grabs Joseph's cloak and yells, "Come to bed with me!" (And you thought the Bible was boring.) Joseph refuses, but instead of being rewarded for his integrity, he is accused of rape by the scorned woman. You can guess whom her husband believes.

Thus Joseph moves from unjust slavery to an even more unjust prison sentence. However, he still does not let his bitterness get the best of him. He approaches his jail sentence the same way he approached his slavery, and because "the LORD was with him" (Genesis 39:21), he is put in charge of all the other prisoners. (Though I'm sure he would have preferred that the Lord got him released.) Nevertheless, we see that the cocky teenager has emerged into a humble leader. Looking ahead in Joseph's story, we wonder if that may have been the purpose for this time.

After some time in jail, two prisoners arrive who have been sentenced for menial crimes. They are the cupbearer and the baker from Pharaoh's palace. While serving their sentences, both have troubling dreams, which Joseph interprets for them. When his words start to come true in their lives, he says to the cupbearer, who is slated to have the more favorable outcome, "When all goes well with you, remember me and show me kindness; mention me to Pharaoh and get me out of this prison" (Genesis 40:14). However, we see in the despairing words of verse 23 that "the chief cupbearer ... did not remember Joseph; he forgot him."

This takes us to Genesis 41, which is the chapter that ultimately reveals the great transformation of Joseph's life. And yet, it's interesting to note that this chapter begins with six small dismal words: "When two full years had passed ..."

Two years of wondering what in the world happened to the cupbearer. *Two years* of continuing to serve a sentence he didn't deserve. *Two years* of wondering why he even had those dreams of stars and sheaths if this was the outcome of his story. *Two years* that end up summarized in a single sentence.

One of the things I've noticed is how quickly things happen when you read (or watch) a story and how slowly things happen when you actually live it. We who are reading know this was only the middle of Joseph's story, but I'm fairly sure it didn't *feel* like the middle of the story to Joseph. Imagining the way he felt after all that happened, it's hard not to conclude he was discouraged. Maybe even hopeless. Yet from our vantage point, we know he is just paragraphs away from life-altering change.

I wonder if this is a tiny glimpse of how God feels when he looks at us.

As I lived in Joseph's story, I realized how limited my perspective was. It didn't change the fact that at this point, at least in the area of relationships, things looked pretty bleak. But it gave me a glimmer of hope that this might not be where things would end up. Somehow this perspective fueled my faith. Though I didn't know what God would do, I had a feeling he wasn't finished. If Joseph was serving a two-year prison sentence with the best chapter of his life dead ahead, what might be ahead for me?

Certainly this was true for my friend Marla, whom I mentioned earlier—the one whose unfortunate marriage crashed around her. There were many points in her story when things looked pretty bleak. After making the painful decision to extricate herself from her marriage, the thought of raising her son as a single mom could not have been pleasant. Nevertheless, like Joseph, she forged ahead.

She found herself divorced and working at a church (which some may consider an oxymoron), but because *the Lord was with Marla*, her church had the eyes to see beyond her label. She went on to have a vital youth ministry, which provided a wonderful context for her to raise her son.

What Marla did not see was another chapter in her life in the area of romance. Where would she ever find a Christian man who would take on her history, become a stepparent to her grown son, and offer her a new chance at love? She couldn't see that happening, and she was okay with that.

"It would take a miracle," she said to me once.

Marla's new five-year-old daughter, loving husband, and grown adult son are proof that God is not finished with our story until we leave this earth. His plan never leaves us permanently in the dark. He always has light in mind.

However, it's important to note that the decisions both Joseph and Marla made in the dark paved the way for the blessings that came to them in the light. Each faced their circumstances with resolve and courage, and *the Lord was with them.*

The Lord showed his presence, not by rescuing them from the dark, but by showing them favor *in* the dark—a reality that both of them accepted and lived out with great courage.

By looking at others' stories, we find courage to live our own story, and we often are infused with hope. But the greatest power of story is when we witness heroism, perseverance, or character, and we're inspired, even for a time, to live our stories differently.

This is what Joseph's story does for all of us. I love that he started out a naive, cocky teenager who thought the world was his. (Think back. Didn't *you*?) I love that as life got harder, he had the faith to do what was right, even though he suffered for it—that even while suffering, he *still* did the right thing. Most of all, I love that the Bible tells us, "The LORD was with Joseph"—whether he was serving as a slave in Potiphar's household or suffering a jail sentence he didn't deserve. Somehow that phrase helps me realize our circumstances aren't always the best sign of God's favor. Joseph's story shows us our circumstances might actually be preparing us for how God's favor will unfold.

That's the hope and the possibility of the middle of the story.

Part III

WAITING
FOR THE LIGHT

There is enough light for those who desire only to see, and enough darkness for those of a contrary disposition.

—Blaise Pascal, *Pensées*

CHAPTER 9

LIVING
IN THE NOW

Be here now.

These three words are so simple to write, but not nearly as simple to live. Especially when we find ourselves in a place we'd rather not be. In circumstances we don't want, we long to be anywhere other than where we are. But where we are holds the pathway to where God is leading us—though we usually can't see that until we look back.

Certainly Joseph found this to be true, for as we read on in his story, we see that his jail cell positioned him for the palace. But he couldn't see that while he was serving his sentence. Thus "Joseph in Jail" can be a metaphor for us when we are living a season we'd rather not live. By embracing the difficulty of the now, we open ourselves to the fulfillment of what's to come—and we can trust that what is happening in our current circumstances will pave the way there.

However, this can become grueling when we are living in a prolonged season of pain or loss. Many of us *feel* "done" way before we actually *are* done, and living our jail sentence with courage becomes increasingly challenging. For single women, the jail sentence can be engagement parties and bridal showers. For widowers, it can be vacations and dinners with other couples. For those who can't conceive, it can be endless baby showers. For parents who have lost children, it can be graduations and weddings. The list goes on, and each sentence is personal. And the very thing that represents loss and sadness for us can often represent joy for others, which makes our sentence even more challenging to serve.

> By embracing the difficulty of the now, we open ourselves to the fulfillment of what's to come — and we can trust that what is happening in our current circumstances will pave the way there.

Where do we find the secret to live these seasons with hope?

Henri Nouwen sheds some light when he says that at every turn, we must open our hearts to the voice of God. This is the voice that whispers to us in the dark, "I have a gift for you, and I can't wait for you to see it." When we listen for that voice, Nouwen reflects, every choice becomes an opportunity to discover the new life hidden in every moment, waiting to be born.[14]

Choice by choice, moment by moment — this is how we live in the now. And one day there comes a moment when we look around and see that things *have* changed. But this moment comes after a hundred seemingly insignificant moments, which we discover in time weren't so insignificant after all.

When I graduated from college, I painted my favorite verse on a tile. It was one of those "promise verses" I had gotten out of a little book:

> "For I know the plans I have for you," declares the Lord, "plans to prosper you and not to harm you, plans to give you hope and a future."
>
> JEREMIAH 29:11

I loved this verse. I memorized it. I quoted it. I lived in its promise. God was going to prosper me, keep me from suffering, and give me the future of my dreams. But if you had asked me what it said before or after this verse, I wouldn't have been able to tell you.

Later, when I went to seminary and learned where this verse actually was in the Bible, I discovered that context is critical in interpreting a verse. It's important to look at what's around the verse to understand what the words mean.

Jeremiah was known as the "weeping prophet," which means that a lot of what he had to say was kind of a downer. This is apparent when you look at other places in his book. It's not uncommon to see phrases such as "I am bringing a distant nation against you ... They will devour your harvests and food, devour your sons and daughters ... devour your flocks and herds, devour your vines and fig trees."* *Have a nice day.*

---

* Jeremiah 5:15,17.

It's just hard to say that in a nice way. But knowing this about Jeremiah actually makes the words of Jeremiah 29:11 even more promising. In the midst of condemning Israel's sin, Jeremiah delivers these words of hope. It appears God hasn't given up on them.

It's also interesting to note that Jeremiah 29 was written to the Israelites while they were in exile. God's promise for a hopeful future was delivered to people who weren't where they wanted to be. This is great news for those of us who find ourselves in that same place.

But perhaps the most significant insight we get from the context of Jeremiah 29:11 occurs just before the verse itself. The promise of hope for the future follows a strong encouragement to live in the present. Could this suggest that the two are tied together?

> This is what the Lord Almighty, the God of Israel, says to all those I carried into exile from Jerusalem to Babylon: "Build houses and settle down; plant gardens and eat what they produce. Marry and have sons and daughters ... Increase in number there; do not decrease. Also, seek the peace and prosperity of the city to which I have carried you into exile. Pray to the Lord for it, because if it prospers, you too will prosper."
>
> Jeremiah 29:4−7

I believe there are some insights in these lesser-known words of Jeremiah that can help us as we live in the now. He begins with a phrase that at first glance may seem inapplicable to our lives: "Build houses and settle down; plant gardens and eat what they produce."

While it's tempting to dismiss this verse as a tip on construction and agriculture, a closer look shows us something more. When I am in a season I don't want to be in, my bags are packed. I have my eye on the door, looking for any escape routes. I am not a buyer or builder during these seasons; I am a renter — and I am barely willing to sign a month-to-month lease. To engage and "settle down" into a life I am not happy with seems incongruous with the future I want to pursue.

And yet in some mysterious way, it's the best way to get there. There may be something God is teaching me, something he wants to show me, something he has for me to do. This is all part of the path that is leading me forward. When I attempt to bypass my present, I hold myself back from my best future, because what's happening now is in some way helping get me there.

To engage and "settle down" into a life I am not happy with seems incongruous with the future I want to pursue. And yet in some mysterious way, it's the best way to get there.

Part of what God is doing may have nothing to do with what I see going on around me; it could have more to do with what's happening *in* me. The Israelites were told to settle down where they were and make a change on the inside rather than seek to leave and change their surroundings. Changing geography doesn't always fix the problem. God isn't just preparing a future for us; he is preparing us for that future.

When I moved to Santa Barbara, I thought God might be

moving me to meet Mr. Right. Instead, I brought my "exile" of singleness with me. However, during that time, my life shifted from speaking to a broad base of people to serving a small community. It was easy to be admired from a distance, but I discovered that you find out a lot more about yourself when your community is close. Those years after my move turned out to be God's premarital pruning, and they proved to be vital for shaping me into what I needed to become.

Jeremiah concludes his thoughts on embracing the present with these words: "Seek the peace and prosperity of the city to which I have carried you into exile. Pray to the LORD for it, because if it prospers, you too will prosper."

If I am in exile, the last thing I want to do is pray for my environment. All I want to pray for is the opportunity to get out. And yet, somehow the last line grabs me: "If it prospers, you too will prosper." When I change my perspective, things start to become what I view them to be, and I benefit from that shift. I may not be able to control my environment, but I can change my environment by the way that I live. This is especially encouraging when we are living in a place we don't want to be.

In the book *Man's Search for Meaning*, Viktor Frankl describes what life was like in a concentration camp. From his studies in psychology, combined with personal experience, Frankl makes an observation about the power of human choice:

> We who lived in concentration camps can remember the men who walked through the huts comfort-

ing others, giving away their last piece of bread. They may have been few in number, but they offer sufficient proof that everything can be taken from a man but one thing: the last of the human freedoms—to choose one's attitude in any given set of circumstances, to choose one's own way.[15]

It is the utmost irony that being trapped in circumstances we'd never want to experience turns out to be the way God frees us. But it's only here that we learn the power of our response. Most of us will never know the horror of waking up in a concentration camp, yet few of us escape the reality of being somewhere we don't want to be. These experiences become our opportunities. When we love where we are, the good that comes from us can often be a reflection of our circumstances. Dismal circumstances call out goodness unprovoked. This, as Viktor Frankl lived to tell, is humanity at its finest.

Living in the now, no matter what the now looks like, gives us the opportunity to claim our freedom of choice. We discover we don't need to escape our surroundings to find blessing. We can create blessing by the way we respond. This is a lesson we can take with us through all of life's circumstances.

———————

As Ken walks through the prospect of death with his beautiful bride, he is aware that every moment is a gift. Therefore, he lives every day as fully and gratefully as he can. Kim often wants to protect him from her agony of sleepless nights, intravenous feedings, and terrible bouts of nausea, which are especially bad when there's nothing left to come up. However, Ken has decided it's his honor to accompany her.

As he lingers in Kim's presence, it's clear that he's decided not to shrink back from his love. Instead he leans into it, savoring every moment he has. He thinks back to the day he promised her "in sickness and in health, until death do us part." Now he lives those vows. In the happiest days and the hardest days, Ken has learned that the present is where God lives. He doesn't want to be anywhere else.

With his lack of control for the future, Ken is fully engaged in the now—and he shows those of us who watch how we were meant to live. He even manages to keep his sense of humor. On one of his Facebook posts about a new "G-tube" that made Kim more comfortable in her pain, Ken wrote that it happily "allows sneaking formerly forbidden treats like 7-Eleven Slurpees, because it doesn't stay long enough for the sugar to be absorbed."

Through Ken's eyes, we are able to celebrate the blessing of Slurpees. And we are the better for it. His response to his circumstances encourages us to be present in our own lives, even when we face sorrow. And we should never stop looking for joy.

This is the gift Kim has given him.

───────⊹───────

This is what the LORD says: "When seventy years are completed for Babylon, I will come to you and fulfill my good promise to bring you back to this place. For I know the plans I have for you," declares the LORD,

"plans to prosper you and not to harm you, plans to
give you hope and a future."

JEREMIAH 29:10–11

Seventy years of exile. That was the "season" the Israelites
were in. God's promise of hope and a future came to people
who would spend the bulk of their lives waiting for it to come.
The future was what they longed for, but exile was where they
lived. They married, they planted, they built, they prayed, and
they learned to "settle down" in spite of their yearning. This
was the lesson God taught them during this time.

So when the promise of Jeremiah 29:11 brought them a
new season, they entered it differently. They were new people
because of who they had become. The Lord's plans to prosper
the Israelites had brought them through suffering, not around
it. Their exile was more than just a detour; it was a critical part
of their journey.

Jeremiah 29:12–14 indicates something else happened
to them before they were called out of exile. After promising
them a new future, God says:

> "Then you will call on me and come and pray to me,
> and I will listen to you. You will seek me and find me
> when you seek me with all your heart. I will be found
> by you," declares the LORD, "and will bring you back
> from captivity."

In exile, God brought the Israelites to dependence on him.
They had been stripped of everything else. There they learned
that an undivided heart was their ticket to freedom.

This can be true no matter where we live, for captivity happens in all sorts of ways. It isn't always what happens to us; sometimes captivity happens in us. When we turn to anything else to receive what only God can give, the thing we are clinging to eventually clings to us. Our choice becomes dependence, and this is a captivity many of us have experienced. Separation from the things we hold dear helps us attach ourselves to the One who holds us. This is an added benefit to the experience of exile.

I think we'll have a different view of our times of exile when we look back at them. They may, in fact, be the most significant chapters of our lives. Our periods of exile have a tendency to call out the best or the worst in us, but they are indispensable to whom we become. I find it interesting that the exile is the only time period featured in the genealogy of Jesus. It is a marker for the coming of our Lord. Perhaps there is hope in this for those of us in exile. We cannot sidestep its importance or the time that we will spend there, but we can live in hope that God will meet us in exile and eventually call us out.

Exile is a place God has permitted. A hopeful future is what he has planned. The challenge before us is to *be here now*. To live where we are, respond to what lies in front of us, and trust that every day, every choice, brings an opportunity to see the hand of God.

And he is leading us in a plan far bigger than we can see.

CHAPTER 10

WRONG TURNS

It was a hot summer day in Missouri, and I was driving with my friend Melissa from the suburbs of St. Louis to a little town called Roach (that's not a typo). I was speaking at a conference for high school students. Because we were several cornfields and a few acres of farmland away from our destination, we turned the volume up on our GPS.

I was struck by the fact that a GPS sometimes gives you too much information. *Turn right in 4.2 miles. Turn right in 4.1 miles. Turn right in 4.0 miles.* At one point, I think I actually threw something at it. Nevertheless, in spite of all those directions, we still managed to take a wrong turn. We were immediately met with that famous GPS word, usually delivered in a woman's voice.

"Recalculating."

Not, "You blew it, idiot." Or, "Where'd *you* learn to drive?" Just a gentle voice telling you in one word that everything was going to be okay. It might take you longer to get there. Your journey might have become a little more complicated, but if you follow your GPS from here on out, you *will* arrive at your destination.

At the risk of overusing this analogy, I have found this to be a little like God. Unfortunately, or maybe fortunately, we are not given a map of our life. Instead, we are given guidance that feels more like a GPS. We don't get knowledge about our future; we are just presented with our next step. And sometimes even that information can be a little foggy. There might be two ways to go, and both like look good options. Neither way is wrong, but you are bothered by the fact that one may be "more right." So you pray. You read the Bible. You get input from a trusted friend. And still you don't feel clear on what to do. But the time comes when you have to decide, so you make your turn.

The good news is that God goes with you. In these instances, God seems to be less concerned about which road you take than about how you live. (Think of it as alternate routes on your GPS.) As you step out in faith and invite him into your decision, he continues to reveal what you need to know and do.

But here's the more radical truth about God: even when you know one way is right and you go the other way, God *still* goes with you. In both the Old and New Testaments, the Messiah, Jesus, is referred to as "Immanuel," which means "God with us." David ponders this truth in Psalm 139:7–8 when he writes, "Where can I go from your Spirit? Where can I flee from your presence? If I go up to the heavens, you are there; if I make my bed in Sheol, you are there." A brief brushup on my Hebrew reveals that Sheol is about as far from the right road as you can get. Some scholars say it's another word for hell. And yet even there, David says, God is with him.

I think many of us feel that if we make a bad decision, God continues down the path we didn't take and we move on without him. But the Bible paints a picture of life as a partnership between God and us. So then the question remains— *What does God do with wrong turns?*

The fact that the Bible is full of stories of wrong turns can be a comfort when we feel we've somehow strayed outside of God's will. Certainly our hiccups make our stories more complicated. And sometimes our complications are due to someone else's wrong turn. But the Bible reveals that, whatever the situation may be, God stays with us in our stories, and he is able to redirect them, no matter how messy they become. Messy stories are his specialty.

In Genesis 12, we are introduced to Abraham, the first great patriarch in Jewish history. The chapter opens with God telling Abraham to leave his hometown and go to a place he has never been. Abraham is told that when he settles in this new land, God will bless his descendants, and they will become a nation with whom God will have a very special relationship. Abraham believes God, but with a barren wife he quietly ponders how these descendants will come to be.

In his mid-eighties, Abraham hears from God again, who assures him that he will still have a son. He goes home to relay this news to his seventy-five-year-old wife. You can imagine the scene. Sarah has already moved well past her childbearing years. Any grieving she did over her failure to conceive a child had long since faded into the past. That chapter was closed.

Enter Abraham with this news.

Maybe at first there was a slight twinge of hope. After all, it was God who promised it. But as time passes and reality sets in, Sarah eventually moves into high-gear planning mode. (I'm pretty sure she was a firstborn child.) She is going to help God make this happen, and God is going to be grateful to have her help. She may have even rationalized that the reason God brought their servant Hagar into their home was that they would need a younger woman to help them with this endeavor. I have noticed in my own life that when I am pursuing my plan, I can usually find a way to spin it into God's idea. In that culture, men having children with servants was a perfectly acceptable route to take. So they reasoned that it *must* be what God wanted them to do.

I've often wondered how much of a fight Abraham put up with Sarah's plan. He was the one who actually heard the promise from God that a son would come from his body. But God didn't specifically say whether Sarah's body would be involved. So maybe, Abraham reasoned, this was okay. There may have been a tiny voice in the back of his brain saying, "Wouldn't God make it clear if this child was to come from a woman other than your wife?" But when he thought about speaking up and stopping Sarah, he remembered — "happy wife, happy life."

So "Plan Sarah" went into effect — and at first it all seemed to work. But then it all went very bad. Hagar, now pregnant, began to resent Sarah. Sarah, now jealous, began to blame Abraham: "You are responsible for the wrong I am suffering" (Genesis 16:5). Abraham, now miserable, just wanted it all to go away. So he tells Sarah to do whatever she thinks is best, still operating under the philosophy of "happy wife, happy life." Sarah mistreats Hagar, and Hagar runs away.

It's a scene that could have aired on daytime television or reality TV (*Real Wives of Canaan*?). But can you really blame Abraham and Sarah for this road they chose to go down? Knowing the end of this story, we tend to judge them for not trusting God enough. But put yourself in their eighty-year-old shoes. What would you have done?

I for one am grateful for this little blip in Abraham and Sarah's great story of faith. It helps humanize them. It's true that their story might have been a bit smoother if this chapter hadn't happened. Some even attribute the entire conflict between the Arabs and the Jews back to this one decision (which, frankly, is a lot to pin on Sarah). But the bottom line is that God was able to take this left turn and weave it into his story, which gives me hope that he can do this with us all.

When God shows up next, he doesn't show up to Abraham; he shows up to Hagar instead. Pregnant, stranded, and left to die in the desert, Hagar is the fallout of this story. She is the victim of Abraham and Sarah's wrong turn. If God hadn't pursued Hagar, his plan for Abraham and Sarah could have continued without complication. Instead, God weaves the complication into the story. God finds Hagar and tells her to come back and bear her child. She, in turn, names God "the One who sees me" (Genesis 16:13).

I love that. When I've made a mess of my life, or my life has made a mess of me — whether I'm the victim or perpetrator of unhappy circumstances — I am never out of his sight.

And so Ishmael is born, and Hagar is vindicated. In the chapters that follow, Abraham and Sarah discover that their wrong road didn't alter God's plan. Grace just recalculated their journey.

———————

When David is introduced in 1 Samuel 16, it is a bit of a Cinderella story. The prophet Samuel is sent to Jesse's house because one of Jesse's sons has been chosen to be the next king. As Jesse assembles his boys, Samuel moves down the lineup of impressive young men, and as he stops in front of the most impressive, he waits for the nod from God. What he hears instead is this: "Do not consider his appearance or his height, for I have rejected him."

Oops. As Samuel continues down the line, there is silence. So Samuel asks if there are any other sons, and Jesse replies, "There is still the youngest ... He is tending the sheep." When David is brought in, Samuel hears God's affirmation and anoints David as the chosen king.

Throughout the Old Testament, we see David's heart for God. The psalms extol his devotion, and the historical narratives prove his allegiance. He is the only biblical figure described as a man after God's own heart. Yet even this man made a very wrong turn. David undoubtedly would have loved to edit 2 Samuel 11 out of the Bible. But it stays — a reminder of the potential liability of human choice.

"At the time when kings go off to war," David is wandering around on his rooftop, and we see from the very first line that David meets temptation because he's somewhere he's not supposed to be. Bored and listless, he gazes down to find the beautiful Bathsheba bathing on her roof. Bathing on rooftops was a common practice in that day, and David could catch a glimpse of anyone doing it if he so desired, for his palace rooftop was highest in the land. Seeing Bathsheba, he is drawn to her beauty, and he subsequently finds out she is the wife of one of his best soldiers. Knowing the soldier is away, David gives in to his temptation and has Bathsheba brought to the palace. The result of one illicit night of sex is an unfortunate pregnancy.

Now David has an even bigger problem. He could confess, come clean, and ask forgiveness from Bathsheba's husband, Uriah. Or he could attempt to cover up his mistake by bringing Uriah home. He chooses the latter. Unfortunately for David, Uriah is too good of a guy to sleep with his wife while his fellow soldiers are engaged in battle, and even under the influence of David's alcohol, Uriah abstains. David then makes a desperate choice: he tells his commander to put Uriah on the front lines of the battle, and Uriah is subsequently killed. Bathsheba is brought to David's palace, and she becomes one of his wives.

At this point, no one else knew the truth of this regrettable chapter in David's life except God, David, and Bathsheba. But God sends a prophet named Nathan to David, who tells him a story about a poor shepherd who has only one sheep, and a rich shepherd who has many sheep—and you can guess the end of the story. After Nathan gets to the part where the rich shepherd takes the poor shepherd's sheep, David burns with anger toward the heartless rich shepherd, convicting himself.

As a testimony to David's heart, he immediately owns his mistake and enters a time of mourning for the wrong he has done. Yet it is clear this is not a turn God wanted David to take. Bathsheba's baby dies seven days after he is born, and though the Bible is silent about Bathsheba's feelings, we can imagine her heartbreak and loss. Movies often portray Bathsheba as a temptress, yet the Bible depicts her as having no choice in her destiny. Like Hagar, she appears to be the victim, hijacked from her own story.

But "the One who sees me" sees Bathsheba, giving her a new story that is prominent in his own. Bathsheba eventually bears another child named Solomon, and he is chosen over all of David's children to carry on his father's lineage. Because of this, she is one of five women listed in the genealogy of Jesus Christ.

We cringe at the extension of grace to the perpetrator until we become the perpetrator. Then, like David, we also find ourselves hoping for a second chance.

But if you look closely at Matthew 1, you will notice she is not listed as Bathsheba. Instead she is listed as "Uriah's wife." This is a testimony that when it comes to unjust suffering, "the One who sees me" doesn't just have his eyes on the living; his eyes are on us even when we die. David's wrong turn may have shortened Uriah's years, but God made sure he was remembered.

It is a great comfort to me that some of the greatest people in biblical history made some colossal mistakes. Maybe it's because I know the mistakes I'm capable of, and have made, myself. In each story, the Bible shows us that God can step in and touch both victim and perpetrator with his grace. We cringe at the extension of grace to the perpetrator until we become the perpetrator. Then, like David, we also find ourselves hoping for a second chance.

And yet, in spite of all this, God doesn't abandon us. Like the father of the prodigal son, he patiently waits for us to find our way back. Luke 15 describes God as a father who comes alongside both the wanderer and the indignant, the one who runs away and the one who loses his way. Whatever shape our wrong turn takes, God has the power to redeem our journey when we let him in. Wrong turns can even become our testimony.

Sometimes, as in the case of Hagar, Bathsheba, and Uriah, we are the victim of someone else's wrong turn. Other times, as in the case of Abraham, Sarah, and David, we make the turn ourselves. But however these wrong turns happen, we can rest assured that we don't have a God who abandons us. We have a God who stays with us in the car. And he is always ready to recalculate our journey.

CHAPTER 11

GOD'S TIMING

One day a man was trying to outsmart God. He said, "God, is it true that a thousand years are like a second to you?"

"Yes, that's true," God replied.

The man continued, "Well, then, does it follow that a thousand dollars are like a penny?"

"I guess so," God said.

The man said, "Then can I have a penny?"

"Sure, just a second," God declared.

God and I have never been on the same schedule. I can count on one hand, if not one finger, the times when he's moving faster than me. I can't recall a time when I've said, "God, I wish you would slow down; you're moving way too fast for me." (Except recently when I look in the mirror.) But the truth is, much of my life has been spent in waits that seemed to take too long. Until I look back and see what those waits produced.

I am someone who journals, and for four consecutive years, I began my journal with the same verse: "Let the one who walks in the dark, who has no light, trust in the name of the LORD and rely on their God" (Isaiah 50:10). This verse became my mantra as I walked through my season in the dark. However, it was the verse *after* this verse that eventually caught my eye: "But now, all you who light fires and provide yourselves with flaming torches, go, walk in the light of your fires and of the torches you have set ablaze. This is what you shall receive from my hand: You will lie down in torment."

They were curious words, and I had to spend some time with them before I understood their meaning. But I eventually gleaned a warning from them that has become a touchstone for my faith.

When I am in the dark, my first impulse is to reach for a light. This verse speaks to that impulse. To sit and wait for God's answer feels counterintuitive to everything inside of me. But it's the only way to leave room for God's move. In his book titled *Let Your Life Speak*, Parker Palmer speaks of something called "functional atheism" — which is when we talk of God's presence, but by our actions we show that we believe the ultimate responsibility for everything that happens rests with us.[16] How many times haven't I asked God for something, and in the time spent waiting for his answer simply figured out how to get it myself?

As more of a doer than a waiter, I tend to put God on a time limit for answering prayer. When time passes and God appears to not be on my schedule, my impulse is to forge ahead

> *Much of my life has been spent in waits that seemed to take too long. Until I look back and see what those waits produced.*

to get what I want. Isaiah 50:11 warns against this impulse. To light my own fire and set ablaze my own torch means I just can't wait anymore for God to act. If I keep waiting for God, the answer I'm hoping for may not happen, for it's already not happening in the timing I had hoped. I see in my path an unlit torch. Do I keep waiting in the dark for God's direction? Or do I set ablaze my own torch so I can make my way out? The answer to this question often paves the road of our faith.

Abraham and Sarah lived this truth, and Ishmael's presence forever reminded them of their ignited torch. However, the remainder of their story reveals God's persistent grace. When we abandon our torches and allow God to light our path, he is still able to take us in the direction he planned. But we have to be prepared that his path might be different from the one on which we were headed. More than likely, it will not unfold on the timeline we've devised.

Long waits produce the best stories. Perhaps that's why God includes them as part of his design. Think of it: when Sarah and Abraham had Isaac, Abraham was one hundred years old and Sarah was ninety. (Thankfully Abraham married a younger woman.) I picture the neighbors watching Sarah's tummy grow, thinking she should lay off the barley. And when Sarah told them she was pregnant, they probably thought she should lay off the fermented grapes. But when baby cries came from Sarah's tent, the cries silenced those voices.

It's the strange stories that become

Faith is believing that God is doing things we can't see in ways we can't imagine. Waiting to see what it will be is how faith is lived out.

God-stories, and their timing makes them what they are. When good things happen when they are supposed to happen, we celebrate. When good things happen when they're not supposed to happen, we worship. A birth at ninety will supersede a birth at twenty-five every time.

But while we love God-stories from a distance, we have trouble accepting it when God has one for us, because inevitably we have to abandon our watches. We have to be ready to embrace circumstances we don't want, combined with timing we wouldn't choose, all wrapped up in an inability to see what lies ahead. But faith is believing that God is doing things we can't see in ways we can't imagine.

Waiting to see what it will be is how faith is lived out.

Drew was only six when his parents divorced, and in those days, children stayed with their mom. Occasionally Drew's mom got him and his brother to school, but she didn't always remember to feed them. She often drank her dinner.

Eventually the school called the boys' father and reported that the kids hadn't been showing up. So their dad came and took them away. Time with Mom was reduced to weekly visits, mostly listening to her complaints. She died a few years later, leaving only a handful of people who grieved her loss. Drew was one of them.

Drew's dad did a good job raising him, but the mother-chasm within Drew inflicted him with a scar that followed him into adult life. Subconsciously repelled by the women who loved him, he was drawn instead to the ones who didn't. A therapist might say he was trying to win his mother back.

After a string of unsuccessful relationships, Drew found faith and worked through his fear of commitment to marry the woman he was dating. He passed out when he proposed. Drew stayed committed to his marriage and helped his wife raise two kids who weren't his. Though he was their stepdad, Drew loved those kids as if they were his own.

Life was not easy, but Drew believed if he did the right thing and kept serving his family, God would bless him. The kids grew up with their biological dad living two continents away, while Drew accompanied them to recitals, soccer tournaments, and volleyball matches. He gave them everything he had.

After twelve years, Drew's stepkids graduated from high school, but then Drew's wife left him for another man. Because he had no blood relation to his kids, Drew was no longer "Dad"; he was just "Drew." And at forty-eight, Drew was unexpectedly on his own.

In the months that followed, Drew discovered (as you will) that God was not finished with his story. There was a new chapter God was preparing in the wings. With all that happened to Drew, it looked as though his life was over. But forty-eight on God's watch was when Drew's new life would begin.

I believe we last left Joseph in the middle of his story. He was sitting forgotten in jail. But after two years, Pharaoh had a troubling dream about cows and grain, and suddenly the cupbearer awakened from his post-jail stupor. He piped up and said to Pharaoh, "Today I am reminded of my shortcomings."(If I were Joseph, I'd be thinking, "I'll say!") The cupbearer went on to tell Pharaoh about a man he met in prison who interprets dreams. And in an instant, Joseph's jail sentence came to an end. An instant plus two years, that is.

It strikes me how quickly things move when God is ready—and how slowly things can go when he is not. That is the challenge of living according to God's watch. However, looking back on Joseph's jail time, we see that the timing was perfect. It was Pharaoh's dream that paved the way for Joseph's power, so Joseph was remembered at the opportune time. From this perspective, the cupbearer was right on schedule.

This is a great reminder for those of us who have had experiences with "cupbearers," those people or circumstances that leave us feeling abandoned, abused, and forgotten. It's the cupbearers that often drive us to take things in our own hands. If we let them, they can hijack our lives. However, we learn from Joseph's story that God is bigger than the cupbearers. He can even use their mistakes to accomplish his plans. Believing that can change everything.

For Joseph, the cupbearer was only one of the many who mistreated him. He could have emerged from jail a vengeful, bitter man. Instead, Joseph gained a new perspective on what happened to him. In the years that followed, we see that God not only used that jail sentence to line up Joseph's circumstances—he also used it to line up Joseph's heart. That's a part of God's timing we just can't rush.

When Joseph's brothers came to Egypt to beg for food, they didn't recognize the leader before them. It was their long-lost brother to whom they bowed. (Remember that dream?) It was a moment that could have been ripe for revenge. Instead, it became a moment for undeserved grace.

Joseph said to his brothers, "Come close to me." When they had done so, he said, "I am your brother Joseph, the one you sold into Egypt!" (In a children's Bible, their thought bubbles read, "Uh oh....") "And now, do not be distressed and do not be angry with yourselves for selling me here, because it was to save lives that God sent me ahead of you." (We *knew* there was a good reason we did that!) "For two years now there has been famine in the land, and for the next five years there will not be plowing and reaping. But God sent me ahead of you to preserve for you a remnant on earth and to save your lives by a great deliverance. So then, it was not you who sent me here, but God. He made me father to Pharaoh, lord of his entire household and ruler of all Egypt" (Genesis 45).

At that moment, all thought bubbles are silenced, and the brothers stand in awe of God's sovereignty and grace.

Joseph now could see a broader view of what happened to him, and he recognized God was authoring a story much bigger than his own. This is true for all our stories. Seeing our story in a larger context helps us to embrace God's timing and circumstances. It can also strengthen us in personal loss. Knowing our immediate discomfort could be working toward a "greater good" helps us trust the big picture of what's happening. It can also give us the courage to wait and see what our discomfort may become.

It's in looking back that we're able to understand the purpose of God's timing. But in the moment, it can be hard to embrace. However, we often thank God in the end for the wait we suffered through—especially when we see what our wait produced.

In many cases, we aren't ready for what's coming until the time it arrives anyway. Certainly Jen and Adam found this to be true. When they first attended the dinner where Shannon and Dave expressed their exuberance about their adoption, they were not yet open to the path God had in store for them. It was a full year before the shift in their hearts occurred.

A look at their baby's backstory reveals the broader scope of God's timing. Caylee had to spend three months in a neonatal intensive care unit before she could be placed in foster care. Ironically, that was three months before Jen and Adam decided to put their names on a list. A week after God opened Jen's and Adam's hearts to receive a baby, Caylee was ready for her future home. They believe now she was waiting for them.

Because we exist on a timeline that God is not bound by, we see things from a limited perspective. Thus we *look ahead* to what God *already sees*. The darkness we experience thinking of our future is not darkness to God because he is already in that future. And he's at work in what we can't yet see. This knowledge helps us wait out our circumstances because we know someday we will look back and see things differently. The reason we can trust God is that he already does.

Perhaps one way to look at it is to refer again to our analogy of a microscope. The lens is a symbol of what we view. Because we are absorbed in the detail of the microorganism, we can't see the big picture of where and why that microorganism exists. Pulling our eye back from the lens, we now see it from a God's-eye view, and we gain a perspective that transforms our thoughts about that microorganism.

Trusting that God knows more and sees more, and that he is pulling for our eternal well-being, helps us embrace his timing — especially when we get a glimpse of what his timing can produce. Looking back on the stories of this chapter, we see that Joseph emerged from jail a different leader. Jen and Adam emerged from their struggle a different couple. And Drew? Well, if I didn't make you wait for something in a chapter devoted to God's timing, I don't think I'd be doing my job.

Instead I will leave you with the words of a lesser-known prophet named Habakkuk (whose name might be the reason he is lesser known). His words capture the essence of what faith looks like when we're waiting in the dark.

> Though the fig tree does not bud
>   and there are no grapes on the vines,
> though the olive crop fails
>   and the fields produce no food,
> though there are no sheep in the pen
>   and no cattle in the stalls,
> yet I will rejoice in the LORD,
>   I will be joyful in God my Savior.
>
> HABAKKUK 3:17–18

CHAPTER 12

LETTING GO

By the time I graduated from high school, I knew I was going to be an actress. I had been a lead in several plays, got an award at a high school assembly, and was accepted into the drama department at UCLA. My career was well on its way.

I planned to marry in my late twenties. I wasn't in the "Ring by Spring" group when I graduated from college. I intended to do a few things before I settled down. Mr. Right would have to wait a bit to fit into my plans. However, Mr. Right somehow didn't get the memo. Either that or he missed the "bit" part when I asked him to wait. Twenty years later, he still hadn't shown up.

You may have figured out by now that I am not an actress. When I got to UCLA, doors stopped opening in that direction, and after I graduated, I stopped knocking on them. I ended up with a degree in theater arts that decorated my wall but had little to do with what I was doing with my life. When I got to my mid-thirties, Mr. Right was not there to meet me, and my 2.5 kids and white picket fence didn't seem to be coming together either. It was apparent my life was going to be very different than I planned.

We've all heard the quote, "If you want to make God laugh, tell him your plans." It's not a Bible verse, but I think I'll vote for it when the next translation comes out. Certainly there are many other verses that carry its sentiment. Perhaps the strongest comes from James 4:13–15:

> Now listen, you who say, "Today or tomorrow we will go to this or that city, spend a year there, carry on business and make money." Why, you do not even know what will happen tomorrow. What is your life? You are a mist that appears for a little while and then vanishes. [*Don't hold back, James. Tell us how you really feel!*] Instead, you ought to say, "If it is the Lord's will, we will live and do this or that."

So, practically speaking, how do we live this way? Are we supposed to stop planning altogether? Or are these verses more about our willingness to let go of the plans we've made?

One way to look at it is to think of God as your editor. He isn't writing your life story for you, but he certainly is writing it with you. An author will tell you their editor is the invisible force behind their book. Editors don't write your words, but they have veto power over them. They often determine which words make it in the book. As I write, I am aware that some of what I intend to be in this book might not end up as what you ultimately read. It's already happened, and I haven't even made it to the last chapter! But thankfully, I trust my editor. Because of that, I can rest in his direction for my book.

That doesn't mean there aren't times when I question my editor. I don't always understand the way he works. When I include something in my book that I really like and he changes it, I have a hard time accepting his change. A more experienced author had worked with my editor on two of his award-winning books, and when I asked him for advice, he offered one simple phrase: "Listen to everything he says. He's always right."

They were words directed toward how I should write. But they're also good words to think about for how we should live.

If there is one book in the Bible that children love, and scholars love to avoid, it's probably the book of Jonah. And it mostly has to do with that darn whale. The big fish is actually a small part of the story, though certainly the most dramatic. The story is primarily about a man with plans, and this man's plans did *not* include Nineveh. Imagine his distress when that's exactly where God calls him to go. The book opens with the Master Editor approaching Jonah's life with an eraser and an arrow pointing in a very specific direction: "Go to the great city of Nineveh and preach against it, because its wickedness has come up before me."

We see how much Jonah appreciated his Editor's direction in the next verse: "But Jonah ran away from the LORD and headed for Tarshish. He went down to Joppa, where he found a ship bound for that port. After paying the fare, he went aboard and sailed for Tarshish to flee from the LORD."

Jonah did what many of us do when we hear something we

don't want to hear—he moved to a place where he could no longer hear it. In Jonah's case, it was an actual place he went to, but not all escapes involve geography. Even when we sometimes sense God leading us in a life-giving direction, we find it hard to pry our fingers from our plans. However, we discover when we ignore him and pursue our plans that God's tracking system has a wider range than we thought. And it finds us in ways we'd never expect.

> Then the LORD sent a great wind on the sea, and such a violent storm arose that the ship threatened to break up ...
> But Jonah had gone below deck, where he lay down and fell into a deep sleep. The captain went to him and said, "How can you sleep? Get up and call on your god! Maybe he will take notice of us so that we will not perish."
>
> JONAH 1:4–6

The God Jonah was running from would not let Jonah leave him behind—and he was wreaking havoc in Jonah's circumstances. So Jonah decided to take a nap. I wonder how many times I've done the same. Maybe it's not literal sleep I've escaped to, but there are many ways to "nap" when God is pursuing me. I simply find a way to lower the volume of his voice.

I do that when I don't like what I'm hearing. Or when God is trying to move me in a different direction than I planned. It could be something he wants me to do or something he wants me to stop, a turn he is asking me to take or one he wants me to avoid. If he's moving me where I want to go, I am happy to listen to him.

It's when I don't like where he's moving me that I suddenly grow deaf.

But I have discovered that God holds the button for his volume control, no matter how hard I try to snatch it from his hands. And he will use whatever alarm he needs to use to wake me up. In Jonah's case, it was a great storm. So Jonah responded the way many of us do when our plans have been thwarted. He was ready to cash it all in. "'Pick me up and throw me into the sea,' he replied, 'and it will become calm. I know that it is my fault that this great storm has come upon you.'"

> *Letting go requires a death of sorts, as we mourn the loss of a life we were clinging to and embrace the dream of a God who is clinging to us.*

Sometimes we'd rather die than obey the voice that's calling us. And in a way, that's just what we have to do. Letting go requires a death of sorts, as we mourn the loss of a life we were clinging to and embrace the dream of a God who is clinging to us. Saying yes to God means saying yes to a bigger life, and he won't settle for less. He doesn't want us to either.

In the summer of 1998, I thought it was my destiny to become a pastor's wife. I had fallen in love with someone who shared my passion for ministry, and I knew God had to be smiling. This had to be what he had in store for my life.

While we were dating, we had the opportunity to go on a mission trip together. It was the perfect way to see how we did as a team. He was already smitten, and this could seal the deal. A ring couldn't be too far behind.

It was my first trip to Haiti, and I immediately fell in love with everything around me. I don't know if it was my state of mind, but it was then that Haiti lodged itself into my heart. After this trip, Haiti and I would never be the same.

Our tour guide was a man named Ephraim. He was a soft-spoken man, and he said very few words as we drove through the slums of Port-au-Prince. He assumed that the scenery spoke for itself. We witnessed miles of one-room concrete homes piled on top of one another and glimpsed children and pigs bathing together in the sewers. As we sat in silence, I observed that our tour guide's gentle, understated personality was paired with a contagious smile that penetrated the darkness around us. He didn't minimize what we were experiencing; he just made sure we didn't miss the beauty beyond it.

Ephraim's sudden laugh as he greeted the children reminded me of the 7Up Uncola man from commercials long ago — a booming Jamaican laugh that instantly filled people with joy. Ephraim was a light in the midst of great darkness, a beautiful spirit who shone with God's love.

I couldn't help but want to know more about this man — where he came from, how he spent his days when he wasn't hosting Americans. He never spoke about himself unless asked, and then only minimally. So I asked a lot of questions.

Ephraim was born on the island of Lagonave, a small island off the coast of Haiti. It was home to the poorest of the poor. He was sent alone with his brother to Port-au-Prince to get educated when he was thirteen, and they were each given one outfit a year, including shoes. The shoes usually lasted nine months. His brother went back to Lagonave after a year, but Ephraim stuck it out. Eventually he graduated, mastered three languages, and became a pastor of a small church in Port-au-Prince. Most of his classmates left the country, but he decided he never would. He lived at his church with his wife and two children, and worked at Compassion International so he could pastor his church for free.

We struck up an unlikely friendship. Though we had different skin tones, we seemed to have kindred spirits. At the end of the week, I told him I would find a way to keep in touch.

When I got back to the states, my pastor-boyfriend and I broke up. Ephraim, however, became a permanent fixture in my life. Through letters, I discovered it was his dream to start a school in his church. He was so heartbroken at the ongoing oppression of his country and the minimally successful intervention from people outside his country that he wanted to raise up a generation *within his country* that would bring about change. With all the problems I saw in Haiti, I couldn't help but think this might be the only thing that could work.

At the time, I was supporting myself and didn't have much to give. I did what I could, but dreamed of more. Nine years later, when I began working at a church in Santa Barbara, we formalized a partnership with Ephraim's church. Once a year we took a team of people to Haiti and raised funds to purchase a generator, a stove, paints, construction materials, books, supplies, and medicine. A doctor from our church fell in love with

Ephraim's ministry and travels there three times a year to conduct health clinics for kids and families. When the earthquake hit in 2010, our church took an offering to reconstruct the areas of Ephraim's church that were damaged. Because of this offering, Ephraim's church became a gathering place for families that had lost their homes. Currently, plans for Ephraim's school are set to materialize before he retires, and some of the proceeds from this book (if there are any) will find their way into his hands.

I think back to the relationship that led me to make that very first trip to Haiti. What a different story I had in my head at that time. It's one of many stories I've written that has been erased and rewritten, made better and bigger, and changed by my life's Editor. And looking back, he did a masterful job.

———◆———

Pastor and author Craig Barnes writes, "God is often silent when we prefer that he speak, and he interrupts us when we prefer that he stay silent."[17] Certainly Jonah would agree. After his brief stay in the belly of a huge fish, Jonah decided to obey God and finally headed to Nineveh (after a bit of a head start from the fish).

When he arrived there, his sermon on repentance was almost laughable. No three points. No exegesis. You got the feeling he didn't want it to succeed.

"Forty more days and Nineveh will be overthrown."

Back and forth Jonah walked through the city, mumbling those eight words—and wouldn't you know it? It worked.

The people repented; God forgave. And Jonah was not happy about it. After all the hell God had raised to get Jonah there, you'd have thought he would have saved some to punish the Ninevites.

Instead, God proceeded to teach Jonah through a vine that grace is not selective. By providing shade for him and then taking it away, God showed Jonah that grace was an unearned gift. In the dialogue that follows, Jonah learns that the God he serves is not exclusively on his team. Because of this truth, God searches for people who are willing to see beyond their point of view, love beyond their means, and trade in their individual stories. It's a sacrifice to be sure. Jonah's pouts point to that fact. But if you are willing to let go of your story, you get to be a part of God's story.

And that's the one that ultimately keeps getting told.

Part IV

WHEN GRACE FILTERS THROUGH

Love falls to earth, rises from the ground, pools around the afflicted. Love pulls people back to their feet. Bodies and souls are fed. Bones and lives heal. New blades of grass grow from charred soil. The sun rises.

—Anne Lamott,
Help Thanks Wow: Three Essential Prayers

CHAPTER 13

THE SURPRISE
OF GRACE

Grace, by its very nature, is unexpected. It's the last thing you think you'll get. It's a party when you expect to be punished, and acceptance when you're used to being shunned. Grace can be new eyes, a second chance, a meal that grows. It's fine wine that comes out late at a wedding, and it's the first laugh after a funeral is through. Sometimes it even interrupts the funeral.

This happened to me at my grandmother's funeral. Because my family was like that one in *My Big Fat Greek Wedding*—only Serbian—every occasion I participated in with them was larger than life. So it came as no surprise that when my grandmother died, her memorial services lasted a week. Thankfully only one of them involved an open casket. I was ten at the time, and it was the first time I'd ever seen a dead body. It was clear to me that the body no longer housed my grandmother, but my great-grandmother, overwhelmed with sorrow, almost climbed in the casket with her. It was my first vivid image of grief.

The grieving continued through the week, and after several occasions of weeping (and eating and drinking) and more weeping, we were finally at the graveside where my Baba would be put to rest. Silently, we gathered around her casket to pay our last respects.

Then, right in the middle of the prayers and incense, it happened. I got the worst case of giggles I've ever had. I tried everything to keep them down. I don't know if I was reacting to being sad for so long, but the more I tried to think of anything serious, the harder I wanted to laugh. I bit the inside of my cheeks to keep myself stifled. Even now, I remember how scandalous it felt. However, looking back, I believe my Baba didn't really mind. Sometimes I even wonder if she was tickling me.

Because when we're in the midst of a season of suffering, what we need most is the interruption of grace.

It was summer 2008, and our book club had just had its last meeting, so I decided to treat my coleader to a bite to eat. He's a low-key guy, so it surprised me when between bites he said, "There's this guy I go jogging with, and when I'm with him, I think of you." I was used to being targeted for "this guy you should meet," but Greg wasn't the matchmaker type, so it piqued my interest. *This guy's* wife had recently left him and was on her way to becoming an ex-wife, so Greg wasn't sure if he was open to meeting anyone. Given my history with ex-wives, I thought it was just as well. Besides, I was in the midst of trying to resuscitate a mediocre relationship, so I wasn't sure if I should get distracted.

A month later, another friend talked to me about the same guy. She then proceeded to invite me to a party where she knew he'd be. I waffled, but at the last minute I decided to go. When he walked into the room, I was glad I did.

He had piercing blue eyes, brown hair, a six-foot-three-inch frame, a great smile, and when he found out I was a pastor he didn't run out of the room. Oh, and did I mention those eyes? I felt dizzy. I was way too old to be feeling the way I did. Besides, I was sure I'd never see him again. At least that's what I told my pounding heart.

Imagine my surprise Monday morning when an e-mail from him popped up on my screen. I was giddy. He asked if I had time to meet him to talk about his stepdaughter. She had stopped speaking to him, and he wondered if there was anything he could do. He thought since I was a pastor I might be able to advise him.

All I could think was that he probably knew some other pastors, and I was just glad I was the one who got picked. I smiled, wrote "of course," and pressed Send.

We met on a curb in front of the Santa Barbara courthouse. I can still picture the scene when I made my approach. He was wearing a yellow button-down shirt, blue jeans, cowboy boots, and a spectacular face. Somehow all of this was wrapped around a sincere and humble personality. I wondered how obvious it was when I started melting into his eyes. If it was, he didn't seem to mind. (Maybe I just hoped that was the case.)

As the scenery became fuzzy around us, I gave him the best advice my brain could muster.

"You've got to just keep loving her," I said. "At whatever level she will allow. She's probably hurt by what happened, and you may be the target. Move slow."

When I finished, I wondered if I was only talking about his stepdaughter.

———————

The surprise of grace leaves us to wonder, *Why here? Why now?* It's a welcome interruption to our questions, *Why not here? Why not now?* And yet we have a hard time reorienting ourselves. We learn in suffering to gear up for sorrow, but we are often unprepared when we are met with joy.

> *The surprise of grace leaves us to wonder,* Why here? Why now? *It's a welcome interruption to our questions,* Why not here? Why not now?

In suffering we learn to clench our fists, and it's hard to break that habit. Sometimes we even talk ourselves out of our grace. When I met "Mr. Blue Jeans and Boots," I felt myself gearing up for disappointment. It was a defense mechanism I had learned by heart. He was too good to be true, so it couldn't be true. I had never been in a script where things actually worked out.

But the nature of grace is that it surprises us. It takes us on a journey we can't plan for or expect. The beauty of grace is that it invites us in to a miracle, and without knowing what's going to happen, we're invited to accept.

This is no small feat when we've been disappointed.

If you were to do a character study on the life of Jesus, you'd end up with "loves to surprise people" near the top of the list. Jesus consistently does what we don't expect. For his debut miracle, Jesus turned water into wine, which frankly seems a little unspiritual to me. I love a good chardonnay, but I'd have thought he'd go a different direction right out of the gate. From there, he goes on to quiet a storm, cast demons from a naked man into a bunch of pigs, take an evening stroll on top of a lake, and turn a single meal into an all-you-can-eat banquet.

Jesus' followers quickly discovered there was no way to anticipate what he'd do next.

He healed hundreds of people, mostly strangers. Yet when his close friend was sick, he let him die. John 11 repeats three times that Lazarus was sick, almost to emphasize that Jesus couldn't have missed it. Even when he was told directly—"the one you love is sick"—Jesus stayed where he was.

So Mary and Martha waited while their brother got sicker. Then they waited longer and watched him die. Still no Jesus.

As it turned out, Jesus was waiting for Lazarus's death for a reason. But all Mary and Martha knew was that their Lord failed to show up. Any miracle they'd seen Jesus do in the past was no longer an option—but what we've seen isn't always an accurate marker for what God might do.

Jesus had in mind something bigger than a healing, and he was willing to bear their disappointment so that God's glory could be displayed. It would be a miracle that would point to more than just Lazarus. He says to his disciples, "Lazarus is dead, and for your sake I am glad I was not there, so that you may believe. But let us go to him" (John 11:14 – 15).

When Martha hears that Jesus is coming, she courageously heads out to meet him. Even in her disappointment, she hangs on to her faith. After getting a bad rap for being obsessed with a clean kitchen, this becomes Martha's finest hour. She believes her brother's story is over, but she has confidence in the eternal story. In this, she proclaims her faith.

As they approach the graveside, Mary finally comes out and meets them. She falls at Jesus' feet and begins to weep. The fact that we know what Jesus is about to do makes his response even more poignant. He joins her in her grieving.

"Jesus wept"* is the shortest verse in the Bible, but its simplicity conveys a weighty truth. It's possible it communicates more about God's heart than any other verse.

Years ago, Rabbi Harold Kushner wrote a book about God and suffering that came out of his personal journey with his son's fatal diagnosis. It was called *When Bad Things Happen to Good People*. His theme seemed to strike a chord, as the book held a place on the *New York Times* bestseller list for months. His premise was that we can love God in our suffering because he is not responsible for it; he simply comes alongside us in our pain. However, to the discomfort of many evangelicals, Kushner took his point a step further and concluded, "It is too difficult even for God to keep cruelty and chaos from claiming their innocent victims."[18]

For centuries, people of faith have tried to reconcile a lov-

---

* John 11:35.

ing God with a sovereign God and end up, like Kushner, favoring one over the other. Yet here, in the shortest verse in the Bible, we see the possibility that both are true.

It was Jesus' waiting that caused Mary's and Martha's suffering. He then weeps with them for what his actions have allowed. We are back to the mystery of Job, as we are presented in the flesh with God's paradoxical ability to be all loving, yet all-powerful—with us in our pain and yet allowing our discomfort, all for some greater picture we can't yet comprehend but are called to trust.

> *There are times here on earth when God does more than weep, when for one shining moment he takes our suffering away. In a way, it's like a giggle at a funeral, a sign of hope for what will one day be restored.*

And yet this story reveals there are times here on earth when God does more than weep, when for one shining moment he takes our suffering away. In a way, it's like a giggle at a funeral, a sign of hope for what will one day be restored.

Jesus asks Mary and Martha to take him to their brother, and they assume he wants to pay his respects and say good-bye. So when Jesus asks for the tomb to be opened, it's an awkward moment. Martha doesn't want a stench to be the last memory of her brother. But she has no idea the memory Jesus has in store—for when Jesus speaks again, he calls out to Lazarus to come and join them.

I like to imagine their faces when Lazarus does what he is told.

Grace is beheld best against the backdrop of disappointment, and it's usually meant for a larger context than simply our own. Lazarus was raised not just for his own life but for the lives that witnessed his resurrection. Reading his story today, we could say he was even raised for us. When grace touches one, it is meant to touch more than one. Grace becomes a movement through which hope comes.

Jesus' miracles didn't solve every human disappointment. They were signs for what God will someday do for us all. Perhaps in that same spirit, our stories of grace are given to us to touch others. The grace we've received is meant for more than just ourselves. Through our stories of faith, God gives people hope.

I wonder how many times Lazarus was asked to tell his story. If you were having a party, he had to be the guest to invite. (Especially if you were going to play a round of "Can You Top This?")

We discover in the next chapter that a crowd showed up to a dinner in Bethany just to catch a glimpse of Lazarus — and Jesus began to draw a bigger crowd as the story got out. That, it seems, was the greater point of Lazarus's miracle.

But the amazing story of Lazarus being raised from the dead could only happen because Lazarus was, in fact, *dead.* It was the dark part of his story that made the miracle what it was. Certainly Lazarus sacrificed to be the target of this miracle, for he would be the only man who had to die twice.

But I am betting Lazarus's resurrection was worth everything it cost him; his sisters were changed by what they witnessed at that tomb. Their deepest grief was transformed into joy by an unforeseen miracle. And they got a clearer glimpse of Jesus when their brother came to life.

In some ways, their glimpse was not unlike Job's glimpse. When God gave him a tour of creation, Job saw the scope of who he was. Just like Mary and Martha, his new perspective cast a different light on his suffering. In both stories, loss became the lens through which God's glory was revealed.

Thus it is our great sorrow—even from a chapter we would have given anything to avoid—that often paves the way for God to thrill us. It is that very chapter that makes us who we are, brings us to this place, and positions us to receive what's coming.

And the darker that chapter has been, the brighter grace becomes.

The next time "Mr. Blue Jeans and Boots" e-mailed me, it wasn't for any particular reason. He just wanted to say hello. I can tell you this—no hello had ever felt sweeter. Or scarier.

Which takes us to the next chapter.

CHAPTER 14

FEARING GRACE

Stacy took a deep breath, then looked at the pregnancy test. She'd felt a little nauseous, but thought it couldn't have happened that fast. She took the test to confirm her doubts. When a faint line began to appear, her heart fluttered and then grew heavy. She was struck by how quickly the heaviness came.

It had only been a couple weeks since they started trying again. Drake's birth had taken a toll on her body, but the doctor felt it was okay. Now she wondered if she was okay.

Suddenly it felt like yesterday that she had held her baby close to her, then watched his face as he took his last breath. The sight of his bandaged chest stayed locked in her memory. Looking down at her belly, she pondered the new life that could be growing inside her. She felt her breathing quicken as she dialed Jon's phone.

When they met for lunch, Stacy took out the pregnancy test to show him. He thought the line was too faint, and probably a false alarm. Part of him wanted it to be. It felt easier to expect disappointment than imagine this could happen for them. Hope was a risk he wasn't sure he should take.

Yet Stacy's body told her that something new was happening, but all she saw before her was the course that had already been played out. The thought of going through it again terrified her, but as the line grew darker during subsequent tests, she knew it was time to see her doctor. Her hopes and fears were realized when he confirmed the results.

Now she had to figure out which one would lead her.

———◆———

Sometimes our greatest fear is the door to where our greatest joy lives, but this means we have to go through that door in order to receive it. This journey is part of God's grace.

When we've believed and then watched our hopes crash, something inside of us grows dim. God wants to reignite our faith in the hope that we have lost. However, when that glimmer of hope comes, we sometimes find it more comfortable to turn it off, snuff it out, and run away. Our eyes have grown accustomed to the dark.

> *Sometimes our greatest fear is the door to where our greatest joy lives, but this means we have to go through that door in order to receive it. This journey is part of God's grace.*

Because hope doesn't come with a guarantee of our desired outcome, we feel we can't risk it. In so doing, we send the very thing we long for away. Our fears convince us that our faith will lead to disappointment, and we create a self-fulfilling prophecy when we let fear win. The way to conquer fear is to walk right through it, a path God calls us to in fashioning who we become. What happens to us is God's chisel at work to shape what's in us. And our faith is the jewel that he is trying to mine.

Because with God, some things have to be believed in order to be seen.

From Moses' perspective, the directions were crystal clear: the Promised Land was theirs. They just needed a strategy for claiming it. Since there were twelve tribes of Israel, they would send one man from each tribe, twelve "spies" who would scout out the land and then lead the people in.

When the spies got there, the land was everything God had said it would be. However, there were a few unanticipated obstacles. The more they focused on those obstacles, the bigger they became. By the time the spies got back, the obstacles had grown several times their original size.

You can hear their fears accelerate as they speak. They start out saying the people are big and end up calling them giants. The cities go from large to impermeable; the land goes from being spacious to man-eating (it "devours those living in it"). The spies transform from being normal sized to "looking like grasshoppers." By the end of the report, the spies have let their imaginations get the best of them, and the escalation of their emotions reveals how powerful a fire fear can ignite.

You can imagine how encouraging these words were to the people waiting to go in to take the land. You can hear their enthusiasm in their response:

"If only we had died in Egypt! Or in this wilderness! Why is the LORD bringing us to this land only to let us fall by the sword? Our wives and children will be taken as plunder. Wouldn't it be better for us to go back to Egypt?" And they said to each other, "We should choose a leader and go back to Egypt."

NUMBERS 14:2–4

Back to Egypt? The mere phrase must have made Moses shudder. In fact, Moses is so overwhelmed with these words, he falls facedown in front of the whole assembly. Who could blame him? After all God has done for them, this is their response? Their community of faith has dissolved into a community of fear.

However, there are two spies who stand alone in their resolve—Joshua and Caleb. Listening to their report reveals what the land looks like when seen through the eyes of faith:

"The land we passed through and explored is exceedingly good. If the LORD is pleased with us, he *will* lead us into that land, a land flowing with milk and honey, and *will* give it to us. Only do not rebel against the LORD. And do not be afraid of the people of the land, because we *will* devour them. Their protection is gone, but the LORD is with us. Do not be afraid of them."

NUMBERS 14:7–9, emphasis mine

Fear moves us back to the known, even if the known is what we formerly longed to escape. Faith allows us to move into the unknown. Even if we can't see where we are going, we can trust the One leading us there.

When we are led by fear, we often choose the misery of the predictable over the risk of the unpredictable. What we picture is worse than what we had. Through faith, we develop a new imagination. We may not know the future, but we can see it differently. This can make all the difference.

Fear moves us back to the known, even if the known is what we formerly longed to escape. But faith allows us to move into the unknown. Even if we can't see where we are going, we can trust the One leading us there.

It's not that "positive thinking" drives our circumstances or controls what happens to us. But the lens of fear can keep us from positioning ourselves to receive all that God has. Choosing the way we see things becomes a bigger decision than we thought.

Certainly this was true for the Israelites. In choosing fear over faith, they sealed their destiny. As a result, only two of the twelve spies entered the Promised Land. (I bet you can guess their names.) What the spies believed ended up being what actually happened to them — and ten of them never received what God intended them to have.

This is the tragedy of letting fear win.

⸻

Faith grows as it's acted on. The same is true for fear. These were my options as I stood at the crossroads of my relationship with "Mr. Blue Jeans and Boots." Part of me wanted to run and never look back. The thought of having my heart broken again terrified me. But the thought of never knowing what might happen was even worse. Was I a glutton for punishment?

Or, in some mysterious way, had my heart become stronger? Since my engagement ended, every breakup had taken a little less of me. God seemed to be putting together the pieces of my heart. Strangely, he had used my broken relationships to do it. Each time I risked, even when the relationship failed, I was a little less scared. I no longer feared a breakup the way I once did.

Fear is packaged differently in each of our lives, and these fears are usually more involved than they appear to be. Underneath my fear of a breakup was a greater fear of abandonment, and that was something no relationship could ever solve. So my breakups were actually part of my healing. In allowing me to stand alone, God was mending me—something I was only able to see as I looked back.

With "Mr. Blue Jeans and Boots," I faced my ultimate test. I had never felt so drawn to a man, but I knew from my history that there was a good chance our relationship wouldn't work out. For one thing, this time I was committed to making sure his ex-wife wasn't just taking a hiatus. As a tribute to his integrity, so was he. At the start of our friendship we agreed he should go back and ask one more time if there was any chance of reconciliation. When he left to do that, the tape running through my head said he'd never be back.

In my engagement, fear had kept me from wanting to seek the truth. This time, fear didn't win. My victory was not in the outcome of what happened; it was in the willingness to let go and trust. In the messiness of life, faith is the only clear trajectory.

Choosing faith moves us forward even if we're frightened. However, fear is stubborn and might refuse to stay behind. The good news is, fear begins to shrink with every step of faith. Sometimes we are called to walk through, rather than around, the terror. But we discover as we walk that we are not alone in our journey.

Stacy did pretty well during the first half of her pregnancy. There were waves of fear, but she grew steadier each week. However, the fifth month loomed as the ultimate test. At twenty weeks, she was scheduled for an echocardiogram to determine if everything was whole in the new baby's heart.

"Like lightning striking twice in the same place" was what the doctor said were the chances of something being wrong again. Nevertheless, Drake's development was the only journey she had known. She could still see the doctor's troubled face the day he told her about her first baby's heart.

During this test, Stacy's own heart was pounding so fast she wondered if it would overshadow her baby's. She couldn't see the screen, so she had her eyes fixed on Jon's face. She watched as he gazed at the floating form of their little boy. Because Jon's eyes were untrained to evaluate whether everything was okay, she searched the doctor's face for any reading. His expression remained unchanged. After several unending moments, the doctor turned and looked at Jon and Stacy. Everything went into slow motion as they braced themselves for his words.

"Your baby's heart is normal. Everything looks perfect."

The words fell on them like a kiss from God.

Three months later, Jaxon Peterson was born. He was seven pounds three ounces, and he required only one doctor. Stacy and Jon cried tears of sweet relief. As they watched him come to life on the three days that brought their first baby's death, they found that sorrow had inexplicably become a piece of their joy—so they gave Jaxon a middle name that would hold them both.

Drake.

I think it might be time to give "Mr. Blue Jeans and Boots" his name. (Mostly because it's getting a little laborious to type it.) When we were introduced, I thought his name was Jerry. When he e-mailed me, I discovered it was J-e-r-e. It was through e-mail that our relationship began its course.

During those tentative first few months, we limited ourselves to a once-a-week coffee; however, we e-mailed a few times a week. It turned out to be a gift to be able to get to know him from the inside out. (In this particular instance, the "out" part was so spectacular that it was sometimes hard for me to find words as I looked at his face.)

Even after I knew the past was tied up for good (and there were no second thoughts), I still tried to keep my heart from jumping in too fast. Communicating through the computer helped. Nevertheless, he was such a great guy that I was aware that if things didn't work out, I would probably get hurt. It was a risk I decided to take. I kept my hands open and moved forward in my faith.

What I didn't know at the time was that Jere was moving forward in his own faith. Underlying his failed marriage was the relationship he lacked with his mom, who had succumbed to alcoholism. She died nearly a stranger to him when he turned seventeen. That loss had driven him in ways he was just beginning to discover. He wasn't sure he had it in him to try love again. But faith grows as it's acted on. And fear loses its stronghold as we move forward in our faith.

You may have figured out by now (unless you skipped chapter 11) that Jere's middle name is Drew. His last name is on the cover of this book.

Right behind mine.

CHAPTER 15

THE EXPANSE
OF GRACE

A changed name and a changed life. These were the outpourings of grace that met me at the close of my forty-ninth year. I pulled out and dusted off the wedding dress that had hung in my mother's closet for six years. I called my gray-haired dad and told him to get ready to walk me down the aisle. He got on his knees and thanked God.

We all did.

Not many girls dream of marrying at forty-nine, but as it turns out, it was the perfect time for me. Had I married before, there would have only been half of me on the altar, waiting to be completed. Because of my journey, I came to this wedding whole, waiting to be loved. The bonus was, there were two men waiting to be loved back.

I left a little something out in chapter 11 when I introduced you to Drew. There was a third child, an "oops" that happened four years before he was separated. So Jere had a five-year-old son when we first met. That was another reason we moved slow, for Jordan's affections were as important as Jere's in deciding whether this union would come to be.

Ultimately, we got the seal of approval, and it happened one Sunday at church. Up to this point we had been sitting apart to stay away from the rumor mill, but on this day, Jordan grabbed his dad's hand and made a beeline to where I was sitting. Snuggling between us, he proceeded to take my left arm and Jere's right arm and wrap them both around his shoulders. I felt the heat of a few curious (and likely hopeful) stares on the back of my neck. Apparently Jere thought it was as close to a proposal as a six-year-old could get, because a couple months later, he gave it a shot himself. In Haiti. Right there in front of the entire mission team, he dropped to one knee and asked me to be his wife.

Four months later, I became Mrs. Jere Short.

The wedding was grand, with 125 people on top of a hill, outside a beautiful home in Santa Barbara. Three pastors presided — the third having flown in from Haiti. Ephraim had prayed for fifteen years for this, and he wasn't going to miss it. All five bridesmaids were in their forties, and one was celebrating her twenty-eighth wedding anniversary.

Threaded throughout the day were inklings of the broken road that had led us to this place. With a child that had come from another marriage and a wedding dress that had been purchased for another day, loss was an underlying presence in our joy. Oddly, it seemed to deepen it. When a spontaneous ovation erupted as my dad and I walked down the aisle, it seemed to be as much an acknowledgment of loss as a celebration of hope. They were two sides of the same story, and they both made the story what it was.

Amazing grace.

———————

In Luke 15, there are three stories Jesus tells when he is trying to explain grace. The first two usually get skipped over because the last one is so famous. But each illustrates a piece of God's heart when something is lost.

The first story is about a sheep that gets separated from the flock and wanders off, leaving the others behind. Because sheep aren't known for their capacity to plan an elaborate escape, this seems to be a story of accidental lostness. More than likely, this sheep saw something good to eat, strolled outside the pen to check it out—and when he looked up, the others were nowhere in sight. The point of the story is that the shepherd goes to find the sheep. With ninety-nine others, it would seem that the shepherd could have let one go. But this sheep is not forgotten. The image of the sheep draped across the shepherd's shoulders paints a vivid picture of God's grace.

In the second story, Jesus illustrates a different kind of lostness. A woman has ten silver coins and finds that one of them is missing. Because the coin is an inanimate object, it couldn't have gotten lost on its own; it got lost because of the actions of someone else. Nevertheless, the point of the story is that the woman doesn't stop searching until the coin is back in her hands. In her relentless pursuit, she becomes the second image of God's grace.

The parable of the prodigal son is about getting lost deliberately—the kind that snubs its nose and runs away to chase what it thinks is best. Unlike the sheep and the coin that "get lost," the prodigal loses himself. Jesus tells of the silent father who hands over his inheritance and watches his son walk away, only to see his money get squandered on wild living. Broke, hungry, and in despair, the prodigal decides to come home. Different from the other stories, which paint a picture of God in pursuit, in this story we find God waiting. Grace is the father allowing the prodigal to bring himself back. And when the son returns, his father runs to meet him.

Three stories of loss. Three stories of grace. Each one is unique in what it gives us, and each one is important in what it says about grace. Like all of Jesus' stories, we find our own stories within them. And sometimes they show us the part we need to play when we live them out.

A few months after Jere and I had settled into marriage, something was still missing. His stepson had been present at our wedding, but his stepdaughter was still not a part of his life. Knowing what it was to be a child of a divorce and realizing his stepdaughter had been through two of them, Jere and I knew the journey was hers to take. We had to give her the space and time needed to take it. Nevertheless, eleven years of stepfatherhood had left a wound in Jere that I prayed would one day be healed.

What I discovered in the months that followed was that

the expanse of grace extends in ways we can't begin to imagine. And in this case, it was as if all three stories in Luke 15 converged to frame it.

Headed down the freeway from Santa Barbara to Orange County, I was lost in my thoughts. I had a speaking engagement scheduled for the next morning at a college in Yorba Linda, and it was my first one with a new name. I was mulling over how to share my marriage joy with the students, as I realized that getting married at forty-nine was maybe not going to be great news for the twenty-two-year-old women in my audience.

Since this was a chapel that included the opportunity for child sponsorship, a portion of my talk was going to be focused on encouraging students to make a difference in a child's life. I came prepared to share some recent photos of my child in Haiti, whom I had met several months earlier. Ironically, I met her the same day I got engaged.

During my talk as I finished the story, I flashed a picture of Jere down on one knee in front of me and said, "So you see? You can have a child and *then* get married!"

Unbeknownst to me, someone began texting in the audience as I showed my picture. I knew Jere's stepdaughter had attended the school a couple years before, but she had long since transferred up to Sacramento. What I didn't know was that she had recently moved back. When her friend texted her that she had just seen her stepdad's picture in chapel, she was only three blocks away.

I stayed close to the stage after my talk because a small line of girls had formed in front of me. After a while, I got to the last one. She had beautiful eyes and a nervous smile. Then she spoke.

"I'm Jere's stepdaughter," she said.

Her words triggered a flood of emotion in me that I couldn't control. I grabbed her and hugged her before I had time to think of the appropriate response a wife of a stepdad should make. The best part was, I could feel her arms around me, hugging me back.

And so it was that a chance meeting between stepdaughter and new wife began to pave the road toward reconciliation. It would be the first of many meetings to come. When I called Jere on my way back home, he wept. Only God could be that creative—to take an unplanned encounter and fill it with purpose. To take brokenness and use it to put things back together.

Once in a while the sky peels back and we get to see what we believe. But it's our eyes of faith when the sky is closed that make those glimpses even richer.

Once in a while the sky peels back and we get to see what we believe. But it's our eyes of faith when the sky is closed that make those glimpses even richer. Maybe that's why God keeps the sky closed. To allow us to develop the sight we need to truly see.

* * *

The book of Job really has two endings. There is the resolve of Job's faith, and there is the resolve of Job's circumstances—and the latter almost appears to be an afterthought. After all Job had been through, you'd think God would rush in with his blessings to reward him. Instead he pauses to hold up Job as an example of faith. This appears to take precedence as God's greatest affirmation.

Before God restores Job's circumstances, he sends him—presumably wounds and all—to pray for his friends. Imagine the picture of diseased, broken-down Job arriving to pray for the welfare of his health-filled friends. It's an image worth locking away, a picture of how upside down God's perspective can be.

Job's friends believed that circumstances were a marker of God's blessings, but it seems God wants to make it clear that only Job got it right. So he holds up Job to them *before* he restores him. This was the real end of the story for God. What happens afterward seems to be the postscript.

In this world, it's hard not to see blessing being defined by our circumstances. For God, it appears to be about something else. The end of the book of Job reaffirms the theology that what happens *to* us is not a marker for God's affections. It's what happens *in* us that he seems to care about most. Our circumstances make up the battleground for our faith.

At the end of the story, it's Job's battered self that God holds up as his prize.

And *then* God restores Job's circumstances. The Bible records that "after Job had prayed for his friends, the LORD restored his fortunes and gave him twice as much as he had before" (Job 42:10).

Still, it's interesting to note that when his brothers and sisters showed up, they came not to celebrate but to console. Their grieving shows us that sorrow is not forgotten when the future brings new hope. Both are woven together in the journey of faith.

I imagine the gains of Job's latter life had new meaning for Job, for loss brings with it new eyes. The "without" gives us a whole new perspective on the "with," and if we've learned our lesson, we hold what we've gained more loosely. Perhaps that's why loss can be seen as gain in the expanse of grace.

Anne Lamott says there are three words that sum up the content of our prayers—*help*, *thanks*, and *wow*. I think she might be on to something. The way I see it, "Help" is what we pray when we can't see our way out. "Thanks" is what we pray when we see what we have. And "Wow" is what we pray when we see God.

It's that third prayer I experienced the day I got married.

In the end, I am pretty sure my marriage will not be the crowning glory of what God achieves in my life. However, through it he showed me that whatever happens in our lives, we should never end the story too soon. No matter how old we are or how late it seems or how much damage has been done, endings can always pave their way to new beginnings.

And so, on November 7, 2009, these were the tender words I heard from the pastor as I stood at the altar: "You are here, girl, and Jere showed, and we're going to get this done today!"

And would you believe it? We did.

This time the bridesmaid dresses were worn. We got to use all of the shower gifts. The wedding dress made it to the ceremony. And the ring bearer came packaged with the groom.

Wow.

CHAPTER 16

THE CAVEAT
OF GRACE

Grace is given so that it can be lived. That was the memo the elder brother of the prodigal son missed. We meet him at the end of the story and discover that while the prodigal is away, he is the one who obediently stayed home. When his younger brother returns, he is dismayed by his father's open arms to receive him. He had forgotten they were the arms that held him too.

Somewhere along the way, the elder brother lost sight of his father's love. Their relationship had morphed into the push-pull of obedience and reward, earning and favor. "If I keep doing the right thing," he thought, "I will be blessed." The father's love had become something he thought he could control.

Enter the younger brother. Fresh from a life of parties and prostitutes, the prodigal comes crawling back. "Now," the elder brother thinks, "he will get what he deserves."

It's not hard to imagine his disappointment when exactly the opposite happens.

In a system of obedience and reward, grace is a game

changer, and it can disturb those who are invested in playing by the rules. All these years, the elder brother assumed it was his good behavior that led to blessing. But on the day his brother came home, he learned something else. As it turns out, the father's love was unmerited grace — free for the taking, kept only from those who keep themselves away. This was certainly not the grace he had slaved for all these years. In fact, it wasn't the grace he knew at all.

Unlike the prodigal, whose return resolves his story and leads to a celebration, the elder brother's story is left unresolved. When the father finds him, he is standing outside his brother's party, refusing to come in. He is unable to open himself to the offering of undeserved grace.

With the prodigal son, the father waited. With the elder son, the father makes the first move. Both responses show the intentionality of the father's love. While throwing a party for his younger son, the father leaves it to go pursue his older son, a gesture unheard-of for first-century hosts. If you were giving the party, you were the last to leave — and you certainly didn't abandon your guests in the middle of the party. However, true to form, the father risks his reputation for love, and his actions show his eldest son the place he has in his heart.

Quietly the father stands before his eldest son and listens as he voices his complaints. He then responds by giving him a new definition of grace. It is up to the elder brother how he will receive it:

"My son," the father said, "you are always with me, and everything I have is yours. But we had to celebrate and be glad, because this brother of yours was dead and is alive again; he was lost and is found."

LUKE 15:31–32

Through the father's words, we discover that when grace is received, it must be given away; otherwise it descends into something very different from grace.

We never hear how the elder brother responds. Jesus wants the "elder brothers" in the audience to do that for themselves.

———————

Grace came to me in two ways on my wedding day. I not only became a wife; I also became a mom. This was a gift to my forty-nine-year-old self, because unless God was going to pull another Sarah-type birth, I was pretty sure I had aged myself out of that possibility. (Not to mention the fact that Jere's "fixed condition" after Jordan's birth would have pushed the matter from improbable to miracle.) So becoming a mom to a six-year-old boy was grace upon grace.

However, the caveat that came with this grace was that the word *step* came in front of the word *mom*—and this conjured up all kinds of Cinderella-type images in my mind. One of my immediate goals was to avoid the word *wicked* being placed before the word *step*.

Through being a stepmom, I've learned that the package our grace

The package our grace comes in includes sifting instructions. We are given it so it can be dispensed. And what's really annoying is that it's not ours to choose who deserves it.

comes in includes sifting instructions. We are given it so it can be dispensed. And what's really annoying is that it's not ours to choose who deserves it. It may include ex-wives and ex-husbands, stepkids and shared kids, in-laws and ex-laws (or would that be outlaws?), and even all the people who are 100 percent blood related. Grace, as we learned from the elder brother, is unmerited and free. It came that way to us, and it's supposed to go out that way through us. So the very best way to hold it is with open hands.

Samuel is one of the most famous prophets in the Old Testament. Two Bible books are named after him, and two kings were appointed by him (including David). But one of the most interesting stories about him is how he came into this world.

Samuel's mother was a woman named Hannah, who was barren for many years before she conceived Samuel. Year after year, her husband would take her to Shiloh to pray and sacrifice to the Lord, and year after year she remained childless. She vowed that if God ever gave her a child, she would give the child back to God.

The Bible records that God heard her prayer and that "in the course of time Hannah became pregnant and gave birth to a son. She named him Samuel, saying, 'Because I asked the Lord for him'" (1 Samuel 1:20). Samuel's very name sounds like the Hebrew word for "heard by God." He was the grace-gift Hannah had asked for, and his birth was the event she had waited for all her life.

So now she held this gift, and she had the freedom and choice of what she would do with him. Would she honor her promise and let him go — living her noble part in the God-story of her son? Or would she cling to him, making herself and her son the center of a much smaller story?

It's interesting to think about what might have happened if Hannah had chosen the latter. We know by the fact that we read her story in a book called 1 Samuel that she didn't. Nevertheless, I can only imagine how difficult her choice must have been. To remember the Giver and not get possessive about the gift.

Because of this, her story becomes a model for us in how to hold grace.

The thing about stepparenting is that you're called to parent a child who technically isn't yours. (At least biologically speaking.) But at the end of the day, that's true about all parenting, since all of our children belong to God. When you are a step-parent, you just get more frequent reminders.

Jordan once brought home his family tree from a classroom project, and on it I saw his mom and my husband, her husband and me, and the variety of extended relatives that came to his mind when Jordan was asked to fill in the blanks. I could see that his family tree was a perfect representation of reality, so why did looking at it make me wish I was on Jere's branch?

Each time things like this happen, I take a deep breath and recommit to my branch. And I try to remember how blessed I am to even be grafted into his tree.

Because Jordan's mom lives in Australia and we live in California, for the nine months we have him, I am full-time in my role. I remember how startling it was when Jere and I first got married, after she moved and I realized Jordan was never going to leave. As a former single woman, it's an adjustment coming home every day to a child when all you've had is "drive-by" experiences in parenting. No matter how long I'd stay with my nieces and nephews or any other children, at the end of the day those kids went home. Jordan *was* home. The first couple weeks, I walked into the living room thinking, "Oh, you're still here!" (Thankfully I never said it out loud.)

But Jordan has taught me to be a mom. I had mentored teenagers, but I hadn't spent much time around grade schoolers. Now I had one around me all the time. After Jere and I married, when I would get together with my friends whose kids were away at college, I would say to them, "So this is what you were doing all that time." You don't really get the time-consuming aspect of parenting until you become a parent—and I only have one child. To those who are parents of multiple children, I bow to you. Parenting is without a doubt the hardest—and greatest—thing I've ever done.

I cook; I clean; I cuddle. I put Band-Aids on skinned knees. I kiss tear-stained cheeks. And in all those things, I thank God for the gift of being a part of something so miraculous—to watch this little boy become all he's meant to be. Then, when his mom comes into town, I pray for grace to be sifted out as I step aside and become Mom #2. My heart grows bigger as it hurts. Somehow I know that if I can keep my hands open, get my eyes off other branches, and stay focused on the branch I'm on, I will be a part of God's story in Jordan's life.

And once in a while along the way, I get a gift that lets me know God sees me. The last one came on Mother's Day in a poem that Jordan, now ten, wrote and gave to both of his moms:

Until I saw your smile, I thought life was boring.
Until I felt your touch, I thought love was dull.
Until I heard your voice, I thought you could never read
*   aloud so well.*
Until I was born, I never thought there was so much joy.
Until we held hands together, we weren't in love.

I think I can do this stepparenting thing awhile longer.

———⊶⊷———

So what happens after the prodigal son's party? The father stands between two sons—the one who ran away and came back, and the one who never ran away but in some ways ended up more distant. Now both have been given the gift of grace. Each of them stands at the threshold of a restored relationship with their father. And each of them now understands in a different way what grace really means. What will they do with it?

At the beginning of the story, the prodigal had taken his inheritance and run away. Author Tim Keller observes that when the prodigal did this, the father endured a tremendous loss of honor, as well as the pain of rejected love.[19]

Normally when love is rejected, we get angry or retaliate, attempting to diminish our affection for the rejecting person so we won't hurt so much. But this father maintains his affection while bearing the pain. We see this when the prodigal returns. By throwing a party, the father puts his extravagant love on display.

Surely his friends who came to the party wondered how this unfortunate father could be celebrating when he had been subject to such ridicule. As the prodigal watched his father's actions, he saw how far grace was willing to go. It's up to him how he will live in response to it. He has become the recipient and carrier of this grace.

The elder brother had the opposite experience. He held his inheritance in strictest obedience and stayed home. He believed that by serving his father, his father would reward him — but his anger at his father's grace proves he wasn't really serving his father at all. Instead, he was serving himself. The elder brother is more like the prodigal than he realizes. His brother may have run away to get what he wanted — but he stayed home for the same reason.

In some ways, the elder brother's relationship with his father is not unlike the relationship Job's friends had with God: *If you live a good life, then you should get a good life.* So what happens when things don't add up? The answer to this reveals the complexion of our faith.

This is the dilemma the elder brother faces at the end of the parable. He doesn't get the party he thinks he deserves because the father doesn't give those kinds of parties. Instead he gets an invitation to join another party — to partake in undeserved grace. This is the only kind of party the father gives.

The invitation pushes him, and us, to decide whether we can live with unmerited grace.

If so, we become sifters of that grace. It will spill out in the messiness of our lives.

For me, that's the context of blended families and step-parenting. On my worst days, I find myself measuring and comparing. On my best days, I realize how fortunate I am. What's mine and hers and theirs and ours gets covered by the unearned grace that even brings me to the table. Suddenly it doesn't matter whether or not I'm the "real mom."

I'm just blessed to be at the party at all.

CHAPTER 17

GRACE UNRECOGNIZED

Looking back, we are often thankful for prayers God didn't answer, for they made room for the ones he answered that we didn't pray. Time brings us this gift. Teresa of Ávila said, "There are more tears shed over answered prayers than unanswered ones." I don't know if that's true, but I can think of some prayers that weren't answered that would have had that effect. *Please let Ryan change his mind and marry me* is one that runs close to top of the list. As I thank God today for what I was tempted to abandon him for yesterday, I observe that grace comes in disguised packages. Not getting what we want is certainly one of them.

However, there are also prayers that don't get answered that leave us with great pain. *Please heal Kim from cancer* is one. *Let baby Drake live* is another. The stories that accompany these prayers reveal that some grace is born through our suffering. Any gifts we receive from it come at great cost. Such piercing loss changes those who experience it — but it leaves new eyes. This is a different kind of grace.

These graces, born through time, help us see through the rearview mirror of hindsight. By looking back, we are able to trace the work of God's hand. The things we prayed for and didn't get are tempered by things we didn't know to pray for and yet received. In many cases, we become grateful for God's withholding when we see what he did.

Unrecognized grace can also give us new faith in the present. It makes us aware that things are happening that we cannot see. The things we are praying for that we haven't received may be making room for something we don't yet know we will need.

Faith is allowing God's silence for what that will be.

You have to be careful with signs. They seem to be best interpreted when you look back. I know this by experience.

I am usually not taken in by prophecies about the future. There have been at least two hundred of them about the end of the world, and since the last one was just a couple of months ago, it's hard not to be cynical. Still, I have to say I was taken aback when I received a personal prophecy. Especially when four months later it seemed to come true.

It was February 2001, and I was speaking at a conference in New Jersey. A woman came up to me at the lunch break and said quietly, "I have to talk to you." Thinking she was going to ask me a question about my subject matter, I stepped aside to listen. She took my hand, and then she spoke.

"I was going to go to lunch, but God wouldn't let me."

Now she had my full attention. She went on. "The Lord is going to bring you a husband."

I looked in her eyes just to make sure she was all there. She was as calm and as sane as could be. Then she continued: "He is going to be a support to your ministry. He will take your head to his chest and protect you. He will love you as Christ loves the church."

Let me just say that at that time, I was working at a Presbyterian church. We didn't have prophecies; we had meetings. Nevertheless, because her words cut straight to the desire of my heart, I felt hot tears stream down my cheeks. I think it was because I desperately wanted it to be true.

Four months later, I met Ryan. A few months after that, we got engaged. I was amazed.

A year and a half later, when we broke up, I wanted to call the lady from New Jersey. It seemed there were a few things in the prophecy that she had left out.

When we look back on our lives, some things appear one way at first, and turn out to be something else altogether. This is true about many of the circumstances and relationships that cross our path. The rearview mirror shows us that the events we are living right now may be viewed differently with the passing of time. Our blessings will hold challenges we never imagined. Our challenges will hold blessings we never could have dreamed. Neither is capable of being fully interpreted until we look back.

As it turns out, the prophecy given to me, despite my nonprophetic background, actually *did* come true. It just happened after it *didn't* come true. And all the stuff that happened in between that wasn't prophesied about was in some ways the most important of all.

That is the journey of faith.

———————✦———————

When Joseph was just a boy, he was told in his dreams that he would one day rule over his family. After being sold into slavery, sentenced for a crime he didn't commit, and forgotten for two years in jail—that dream was fulfilled. In between, Joseph lived the journey of faith.

When he finally moved from being a prisoner in a dungeon to being the head of Pharaoh's palace, he married a woman named Asenath, who was the daughter of Potiphera. I know a lot of Egyptian names were similar in those days, but given Joseph's history with Potiphar's wife, this seems like a coincidence too interesting not to mention.

However, what's more noteworthy is what Joseph named his children.* His firstborn he named Manasseh, derived from the Hebrew word for "forget." His second child he named Ephraim, which sounds like the Hebrew word for "twice fruitful." Through the names he gives his sons, Joseph describes his journey through suffering. In so doing, he gives us insight into our own.

When Joseph names Manasseh, he says, "It is because God has made me forget all my trouble and all my father's household." Through this phrase, Joseph alludes to the fact that

---

* Genesis 41:51–52.

some of his sufferings have been absolved by the events that followed it. His difficulties have been reframed in light of the bigger picture of his life.

Most of us can think of events that seemed tragic at the time but that we now thank God for, because they led to a blessing we could never have imagined at the time. When Joseph named his first son, it seems as though he had those sufferings in mind.

However, when Joseph names his second son, he says something very different. Calling him Ephraim, he says, "It is because God has made me fruitful in the land of my suffering."

By stating his current location as "the land of my suffering," Joseph alludes to the fact that some of his sufferings have stayed with him. The separation from his family and homeland had left an indelible mark of sadness on his life. When he is finally reunited with his brothers in Egypt, he has lost many years. Those years, along with Joseph's former self, will never be returned.

Some of our sufferings are forgotten as time transforms them into blessings. Some of our sufferings are never forgotten, and their purpose is to transform us.

Instead, Joseph has become a "new self." His journey to become Egypt's prince has transformed him in ways seen and unseen. The sufferings that have stayed with him have enlarged his heart, moving him from self-centered teenager to benevolent leader.

In "the land of my suffering," Joseph has been changed, and his son Ephraim would forever remind him of that fact.

We see through Joseph's sons that some of our sufferings

are forgotten as time transforms them into blessings. Some of our sufferings are never forgotten, and their purpose is to transform us.

Yet even with these insights on suffering, when I am confronted with some of the sufferings of people around me, I fall short of understanding it. When I read about a thirteen-year-old Cambodian girl who is sold into sex slavery by her parents to feed the family, or when I see my friend with three kids and ovarian cancer come to church in her wig, I am silenced in the face of suffering. There are no simple explanations for the sufferings some people are called to endure.

There is only the comfort that, when it comes to suffering, we have a God who put himself at the top of the list.

———◆———

In 2004, the movie *The Passion of the Christ* was released in theaters all over the country. It provided a graphic illustration of Jesus' journey to the cross. Critics predicted box office disaster. It was bloody, brutal, and raw, and many found it nearly impossible to watch. Yet as it turns out, there were a great deal more who found it impossible *not* to watch. The movie took in six hundred million dollars and ironically became the highest grossing R-rated film of all time.

What was the draw of this film? Perhaps it was the visceral reminder of the answer to the question, "Is there anybody out there who cares?" Somehow it struck a chord, and I can only imagine that the chord was human suffering. I have forced myself to sit through it twice, and each time it's been a tremendously unpleasant, oddly therapeutic, and dramatically jolting experience to help me remember what the Son of God went through on our behalf.

Some critics of the film said the violence "obscured the message," which seems paradoxical to me, as the violence in many ways *was* the message. For those who have truly suffered, the violence of the cross holds our faith. Our hope, illustrated in the last five minutes of the film, is what lies beyond it.

One of the great martyrs of the Christian faith, the German pastor Dietrich Bonheoffer, reflected from a World War II prison camp that "Christ helps us, not by virtue of his omnipotence, but by virtue of his weakness and suffering."

He goes on to write, "Man's religiosity makes him look in distress to the power of God in the world ... The Bible directs man to God's powerlessness and suffering."

He then concludes his thoughts, written just before he was executed: "Only a suffering God can help."[20]

The unedited violence of the cross might be the only thing that can bring peace to human suffering. Through his actions God says what no words ever could. We recognize that grace can come through our suffering. Looking at the cross helps us recognize the cost of grace.

———— ✦ ————

Life reveals that suffering is often the context for great joy. We see this from the beginning, as the cries of a mother's pain brings forth the cries of a baby's first breath. And when we look back on life, we observe a familiar pattern: many of our greatest joys came from our deepest sufferings, almost as if both need to be there for either to be experienced in full. Joy and suffering together make up the fabric of human life.

Perhaps this is best noted by the fact that just as one day we were born, one day we, along with the people we love, will die. It's a fact we may try to ignore, put off, medicate, or develop amnesia about, but it's an inevitable part of our human experience. Because life inevitably includes loss and suffering, faith must take root in this context.

In Jesus' death on the cross, we find a place for our suffering. But his resurrection gives us something beyond our sufferings. The hope of new life is the gift of our faith.

It's a gift that we are told will meet us after death. But it's also a gift that we can begin to experience in life. By embracing the dark seasons of our lives, we can see that endings lead to beginnings, sufferings can lead to joy, and old lives can be transformed into new ones. But we must enter the dark in order to see what lies beyond it. Rather than try to avoid it, we enter its pain.

In the darkness, we are given the gift of discovering a bigger faith. The risk God takes is that we will never see past our struggle to find it.

This is not an easy course, as the darkness brings hurt and sorrow and unmet longings that may seem incompatible with our faith. But God wants to grow our faith to include those things. And more importantly, to experience the treasure that can be found in them.

When we are presented with this opportunity, it can feel at first like God doesn't like us. Because our former faith was contingent on our happiness, the transition to a deeper faith may feel like loss. We have to say good-bye to the faith we had.

As we make this journey, we may brood and mourn and question, and as we've seen from Job, that is okay with God. We may get some questions answered, but we learn to live with many unanswered ones. Like Job, we grow silent as our perspective of God grows.

Our faith is weaned as it sits in the dark.

Then, sooner or later, a glimmer of light comes — not absolving the darkness, but entering it. And we find our faith now has the capacity to move from darkness into light and back again, because we now have a faith that is actually bigger than darkness and light. It is no longer ruled by our circumstances; it has the power to transcend them.

In the darkness, we are given the gift of discovering a bigger faith. The risk God takes is that we will never see past our struggle to find it.

It appears that for God, this risk is worth the prize.

You are that prize.

EPILOGUE

For one night, the man was all alone. He had been traveling with his family, but he sent them on ahead because he needed some space to gather his thoughts. As he mulled over his past, he tried to picture what lay ahead. Doing so made him feel anxious — not the good kind, but the kind a person feels when he is about to confront something he dreads.

All his life Jacob had struggled with control, grabbing at it when it eluded him, sacrificing relationships to keep it in his grip. His only brother had been part of the fallout. Now, for the first time in twenty years, he was about to meet him again face-to-face. The thought of it made him feel tense.

With two marriages and twelve children, Jacob lived a life that revealed the elusive nature of control. Like most men, he had originally wanted one wife and the normal amount of children that would come with her. Like many men (and women for that matter), Jacob didn't exactly get what he had planned.

But no matter the circumstances Jacob was forced to adapt to, they never seemed to alter his strategy. Control was the only approach he knew, and it was that approach Jacob continued to take. Lying in the silence, he mulled over the gifts he had sent to his brother to bribe him for his forgiveness.

Suddenly, Jacob realized he was not alone. A large opaque figure stared down at him with an expression that appeared both ominous and inviting. Was he dreaming?

"Get up, Jacob," the deep voice whispered.

Before Jacob could see who it was, he lunged at the stranger out of instinct, pinning him to the ground. The figure pushed him off, and in an instant, Jacob was beneath him, staring deep into his eyes.

"Why are you fighting me?" the stranger asked in a way that made Jacob feel the question was bigger than it sounded.

Jacob threw the man off and pinned him again. On and on they wrestled through the night, and when daybreak came, they both lay exhausted on the ground. Slowly the stranger got up and started to walk away. As he studied the figure, Jacob was able to confirm what he suspected.

This was no earthly creature he had been wrestling.

"Wait!" Jacob said. The figure stopped.

Jacob lunged at him one final time, locking him in a hold. This time, the figure didn't move.

"I will not let you go unless you bless me," Jacob whispered.

The audaciousness of that request was only surpassed by the surprise of what happened next. The figure did what Jacob asked. He reached out and touched Jacob, the searing power of his finger leaving a limp in Jacob's body, penetrating his soul.*

Looking at Jacob's life afterward, it was evident he carried a grace in his behavior and life that he did not have before. His heart grew through his struggle. His faith had matured.

---

* The story is found in Genesis 32:22–32.

The Jacob that emerged after the wrestling match reveals the mystery of God's touch. It seems the limp he received didn't just come with his blessing.

It was part of it.

ACKNOWLEDGMENTS

This book represents a new chapter in my writing, and for this opportunity, there are several people to thank.

My Ocean Hills family—especially Stacy and Jon Peterson, Shannon and Dave Neels, Jen and Adam Wilson, and Ken and Kim Kihlstrom. Your stories will now live to encourage people you'll never know.

Marlo Blanford, Stacy Sharpe, Melissa Johnston, Vicki Stairs, and Teri Vogeli—who read and encouraged, cheered and supported. Thank you for walking with me in this journey.

Philip Yancey and Earl Palmer, whose insights have infused my mind and heart, and are reflected on these pages.

My "big fat" Serbian family, including Judy and Ty who had me, Chip and Tom who grew up with me, and all the wonderful steps, halves, and extensions to the Polich clan who make my family of origin colorful, complex, and full of love.

To the youth workers who will take the leap from *Help, I'm a Small Group Leader* to *Finding Faith in the Dark*, I hope I can serve you in a new way. Special thanks to Jim Burns, who helped me take that leap. And to Tic, Duffy, Helen, Doug, Efrem, Dave, Marv, Les, Chap, and Mike (who winks from above)—you represent a joyous and fruitful season of my life.

My new team at Zondervan, including John Sloan, Dirk Buursma, and Londa Alderink, for their counsel, creativity, and support.

And a special thanks to John Sloan, who with the help of Greg Johnson took a risk on a youth ministry author that I hope will pay off.

NOTES

1. C. S. Lewis, *The Horse and His Boy* (1954; repr., New York: HarperCollins, 1994), 165.
2. C. S. Lewis, "The Efficacy of Prayer," in *The World's Last Night: And Other Essays* (1952; repr., New York: Harcourt, 2002), 10.
3. Ibid., 9, emphasis added.
4. Philip Yancey, *Disappointment with God: Three Questions No One Asks Aloud* (Grand Rapids: Zondervan, 1998), 57.
5. Douglas John Hall, *God and Human Suffering: An Exercise in the Theology of the Cross* (Minneapolis: Fortress, 1987), 156.
6. Frederick Buechner, *The Alphabet of Grace* (New York: HarperCollins, 1989), 47.
7. Yancey, *Disappointment with God*, 215–16.
8. C. S. Lewis, *Reflections on the Psalms* (New York: Harcourt, 1958), 138.
9. C. S. Lewis, *The Problem of Pain* (New York: Macmillan, 1956), 81.
10. Henri Nouwen, *Here and Now* (New York: Crossroads, 1994), 22.
11. Gerald Sittser, *A Grace Disguised: Expanded Edition* (Grand Rapids: Zondervan, 2004), 76.
12. C. S. Lewis, *Prince Caspian: The Return to Narnia* (1951; repr., New York: HarperCollins, 2002), 150.
13. Ibid., 148.
14. Nouwen, *Here and Now*, 16.
15. Viktor Frankl, *Man's Search for Meaning* (New York: Touchstone, 1984), 75.
16. Parker Palmer, *Let Your Life Speak* (San Francisco: Jossey-Bass, 2000), 88.
17. Craig Barnes, *When God Interrupts: Finding New Life through Unwanted Change* (Downers Grove, IL: InterVarsity, 1996), 135.
18. Harold S. Kushner, *When Bad Things Happen to Good People* (1981; repr., New York: Random House, 2001), 49.
19. Timothy J. Keller, *The Prodigal God: Recovering the Heart of the Christian Faith* (New York: Dutton, 2008), 20.
20. Dietrich Bonhoeffer, *Letters and Papers from Prison* (New York: Touchstone, 1997), 361.